Christmas in the South

Christmas in the South

...

Holiday Stories from the South's Best Writers

...

Edited by
CHARLINE R. McCORD
and
JUDY H. TUCKER

Preface by
KAYE GIBBONS

Illustrated by
WYATT WATERS

ALGONQUIN BOOKS OF CHAPEL HILL 2004

Published by
ALGONQUIN BOOKS OF CHAPEL HILL
Post Office Box 2225
Chapel Hill, North Carolina 27515-2225

a division of
WORKMAN PUBLISHING
708 Broadway
New York, New York 10003

Printed in China.
Published simultaneously in Canada by Thomas Allen & Son Limited.
Design by Anne Winslow.

Library of Congress Cataloging-in-Publication Data
Christmas in the South: holiday stories from the South's best writers / edited by
    Charline R. McCord and Judy H. Tucker; preface by Kaye Gibbons; illustrated by
    Wyatt Waters.— 1st ed.
        p. cm.
    Contents: Preface / by Kaye Gibbons—Introduction / by Charline R. McCord and
    Judy H. Tucker—An unsent letter / by Silas House—What child is this? / by
    Doris Betts—Good will toward men / by Clyde Edgerton—Christmas on
    Madewell Mountain / by Donald Harington—The perfect tree / by Carolyn
    Haines—The gift of lies / by Nanci Kincaid—Largesse / by Gail Godwin—The
    blue carcoat / by Jill McCorkle—Ponies for Christmas / by Michael Knight—
    Christmas holidays / by Ellen Douglas—Merry Christmas, Scotty / by Larry Brown.
        ISBN 1-56512-448-0
        1. Christmas stories, American.   2. Short stories, American—Southern
    States.   3. Southern States—Social life and customs.   I. McCord, Charline R.
    II. Tucker, Judy H.
    PS648.C45C4485 2004
    813'.0108334—dc22   2004048324

10 9 8 7 6 5 4 3 2 1
First Edition

Contents

Preface

CHEERFUL, OVER-ACHIEVING adults and small children seem to get a consistent bang out of the Christmas holidays, but for the lot of us, it is more like a series of days we annually, earnestly endure in the hope that our communal family peace and our individual peace of mind will be intact at the end of the year. Particularly in the South, where major portions of our landscape are never going to match the customary greeting-card depiction of a romantic ride in a one-horse open sleigh, where only a few states are ever carpeted with enough snow to build a reasonably sized snowman, we tend to anticipate Christmas with more longing than most people. And it is more than our temperate weather that has modern Southerners craving holiday perfection. As so gorgeously recounted in this collection, Christmas has become symbolic of the contemporary distance between the old ideal of the traditional, close-knit family gathering together over the holidays and becoming even closer and the newer reality of the farther-flung family separated by state rather than county lines, by socio-political ideologies, by basic values rather than trivial differences, gathering together and either forgiving or becoming more estranged.

We labor to create an ideal and then we guard it against wreckage, sometimes worrying the joy out of the season and ourselves. We want wonder and bliss and the magic of the season, and then we monitor, chastise, and control. We can create battlefields of longing, and when it's all over, we clean up and wait until next year, when we can try for perfection again. It is little wonder that a day so burdened with anticipation and dread so often fails to produce unmitigated pleasure, and that even the slightest mishaps or misdeeds, things easily ignored the rest of the year, are able to make permanent impresses on our memories. The memory treats Christmas different, assigns events a higher value; and so then, given the urgent place of memory in the work of each writer in this volume, it is understandable that each of their stories seems so naturally alive and true that the reader feels instantly let inside and shown around different homes, different worlds, variously decorated with varieties of trees, with love, loss, and longing.

These stories are opportunities for us to consider why the holidays are days we can't wait to get here or can't wait to leave, or both. They are gifts of language and memory that will compel us to regard Christmases past and wonder at the best and the worst of them. As strange as it may sound to say that one of the most beautiful aspects of the collection is the way these writers deal with loss and grief, I say it because as I read, I was washed over with what I suppose one could call nostalgia for the love of my grandfather, who died on Christmas Eve of 1965. His seven sons and daughters and all their children were gathered around his chair, watching him open presents. My mother, Shine, was sitting on his lap. Her long legs hung over his knees. My memory has him pressing his hands to his chest and dying instantly. All the children are herded upstairs by screaming aunts. I will always be grateful to my memory for eliminating any other unbearable events of that day, and I am grateful to the writers for opening the door to my grandfather's house again, where love and joy were so abundant.

I am also grateful to these writers for reminding me, quite literally, of why I love to write. The gifts of Doris Betts, Clyde Edgerton, Donald Harington, Nanci Kincaid, Carolyn Haines, Gail Godwin, Jill McCorkle, Ellen Douglas, and Larry Brown are treasures I have kept stored for use in my own work for almost twenty years. Their humor and pathos, their ability, willingness, and what Walker Percy probably would've called a "knack" for addressing the highest, most important elements of human thought and emotion—love, pride, grief, loneliness, despair, faith, gladness—in the confident and clear cadences of the vernacular, are as evident in these representative stories as in any other of their works.

Finding Eudora Welty's confluence, that place where two different ideas come together and flow as one, is what these writers do best and is what has earned them international reputations as masters of their craft. A reader in France, for example, knows that when he reads "Merry Christmas, Scotty" or any other story by Larry Brown, he is going to meet an ordinary citizen, probably of Mississippi, who is going to use his own unvarnished voice to tell him an utterly profound, extraordinary story that will leave him feeling ragged and redeemed. If these writers used the vernacular to recast only local trivialities, then they would not be great, they would not be who they are; but they are in the habit of using the voices of their particular places to examine the widest and deepest emotions we share, and that is what lifts the best writing of the South up out of this time and place. That these remarkable authors have given us stories about the miracles of love and loss at Christmas only adds another dimension to their art.

Although stylistically different, Silas House and Michael Knight both write with an uncanny grace and authority. Their particular turns of phrase and their ability to summarize the humanity or lack of humanity in a character by one swift or metaphorical movement are feats no writer ever takes for granted, no matter how long he or she has been writing. Like the other writers who have been gathered here to tell us something about the mystery of Christmas, they bring us their singular attitudes, their rich voices, and we expect and receive nothing less than magic from them. One book this full of so much glorious language may, in fact, be the closest thing to experiencing a perfect Christmas any of us find this year. The book doesn't need wrapping either, as it was wrapped around with all our voices, dreams, and wishes the moment the writers decided to give us all such magnificent gifts of their spirit.

—*Kaye Gibbons*

Introduction

WHEN WE BEGAN to gather stories for *Christmas in the South,* we had already agreed on the criteria. First, the stories had to invoke the spirit of the holiday season; second, they had to be authored by Southerners; and third, they had to be great stories.

It should have been easy to make the selections, yet we found ourselves once again asking the same questions: What makes a story a Christmas story? Must it mention the word Christmas, or is it enough to be set in the winter with its short days and quick cold snaps? Must it be as warm and glowing as a Yule log, or might it be as dark as a roux left unattended on the stove?

While that issue simmered on the back burner, we moved on to the task of finding Southern writers. This quickly morphed into the question of who is or is not a Southerner. Some folks think a Southerner is anybody whose ancestors fought for the Confederacy in the War Between the States, as we call it. Others think they qualify if they got moved below the Mason-Dixon Line by IBM and have since learned the difference between fixing to do something and going right ahead and doing it. Does it make you a Southern writer, for example, if you spent a semester at Ole Miss studying under Barry Hannah? We sincerely hope so. Eudora Welty, who was born and lived most of her life in the heart of Dixie, said she sometimes felt like an outsider because she "could never talk about the old family home that was burned during the Civil War." She was a first generation Southerner, raised by a father from Ohio and a mother from the mountains of West Virginia. Maybe this distance enabled her to see her neighbors from some comfortable middle ground, halfway between familiarity and total objectivity. We hasten to add that Miss Welty would be acceptable by all our measures had we not further narrowed our search for writers to those working at the present time.

In the end, the last requirement for these Christmas stories proved to be the hardest to pin down. Miss Welty gave us a standard when she discussed her own short stories in a 1942 interview with Robert Van Gilder: "I'd like people to be moved, to feel they have passed through some experience with me," she said.

It is our hope that as readers pass through the experiences contained in the eleven stories in this collection, they will also experience the magic of Christmas in all its complexity. For Christmas is undoubtedly the most conflicted time of year, so regular, so seemingly predictable—yet so very irregular and unpredictable. It is a time of great expectations, great revelations, and, sometimes, of overwhelming disappointment. The stories that follow exhibit with genuine fidelity the mix of experiences and emotions that constitute the Southern Christmas. We open with Silas House's story, "An Unsent Letter," wherein a young woman from the mountains of Kentucky is facing her first Christmas away from home. "What

Child Is This?" by Doris Betts is a story of courageous nurturing. Clyde Edgerton's "Good Will Toward Men" reveals that good will isn't necessarily a given at Christmas — not unless someone's threatening to expose us. In Donald Harington's "Christmas on Madewell Mountain," a young girl prepares to spend Christmas alone; and in Carolyn Haines's "The Perfect Tree," a sister reluctantly grants her brother's final request. Nanci Kincaid's "The Gift of Lies" proves that well-intentioned prevarication is sometimes a necessary gift, and Gail Godwin's "Largesse" reveals what happens when a young girl is seduced by the material riches of her wealthy, childless aunt. A Christmas parade is central in Jill McCorkle's coming-of-age story "The Blue Carcoat," and duplicitous gifts are called for in Michael Knight's "Ponies for Christmas." A precocious child learns much about her family while pretending to read in Ellen Douglas's "Christmas Holidays," and our closing story, Larry Brown's "Merry Christmas, Scotty," demonstrates that one doesn't really need fancy trappings to enjoy Christmas.

In this age seemingly given over to fancy trappings and total saturation television, we are pleased to report that the Christmas story is alive and well and vigorously plundering every known human experience and emotion. We found an abundance of material from which to choose these fine-spun holiday stories, stories which allow the reader to experience the variety of unfolding dramas that make up the regular, yet totally unpredictable Christmas in the South.

Merry Christmas, you-all!

—*Charline R. McCord and Judy H. Tucker*

Christmas in the South

An Unsent Letter

by Silas House

Dear Louise,

It is peppering snow here in the big city of Dayton, and I had to take pen in hand because while I was looking out the window just now, I seen your face come up plain as day on the glass. I could see you and Granny and Wanda and everybody back home, just like you all were standing out there waving to me. I wonder is it snowing back there on little Free Creek, and has anything at all changed since I left that place? You are a good hand to take a picture. Why don't you ever stand at the mouth of the holler and take one of all the little houses and the mountains sloping down on either side and send it to me? Soon as I get home, first thing I am going to do is stand in the middle of the road and look at each thing for as long as I can. I wish I had done that before we left there, to freeze it in my head the way you can do the sun when you look at it long enough, imprinting it on the backs of your eyelids. But I thought I was off on me a big adventure and nothing like that ever crossed my mind.

Eleshia is doing just fine. Other day we was downtown and this schoolbus pulled up to let a bunch of high school kids off. There was a girl who had on a red coat, just like yours, and shiny brown hair and even had pennies in her loafers, like you wear. Well, Eleshia started hollering Aunt Louise! Aunt Louise! to the top of her lungs. She cried and cried because of course the girl didn't turn around. She thought for sure it was you. Other than that she has done good, moving up here, and has lots of little friends her own age to play with here in our building.

Tell Granny that I got that big jar of molasses she sent me and it melted in my mouth it was so good. I didn't go down to the post office till late that evening (they stay open till six o'clock here!) and we had done eat supper, but soon as I got that jar, I come straight home and made a pan of biscuits. Our best friends up here, Patty and Darrel, was over at the house playing rummy with me and Simeon (they are from West Virginia and exactly like us—you would love them to death and I don't know what I'd do without them), so we all four set there and eat that whole big jar of molasses. We will all burn for gluttony, no doubt. But we had a ball and it was like tasting home right on our lips. It must have cost Granny a war pension to mail that big thing. I know jar and all weighed a good two pound.

Your last letter liked to have tickled me to death. I laughed till I come one ace of peeing on myself. I read parts of it to Simeon, who said you ought to be in a show you're so funny. He says you make for way more laughs than Lucille Ball. I miss your sweet, smooth voice so much, and wish you could put that in a parcel and mail it to me. There is a record store up here where you can go right in a booth and make a record of your own voice. Maybe someday we will have one of them at home, but by then you will be a famous singer just like Loretta Lynn, mark my words. Have you heard her new song? I love it. I still can't get over her being from Johnson County. Why, she's practically our neighbor and you know we're probably kin. Everybody in Crow County is kin to Johnson County people somehow or another. There is a real good country station up here that we listen to all the time. It surprised me they even listened to country up here. I thought only mountain people liked it, but northern people eat it up.

Well, to tell you the truth, I have been beating around the bush in this letter so far. I'll just come right out and say it. It is ten days till Christmas and I think that I will die up here. I hate to send you a letter with sad news but if I don't put this down on paper I know that I will die from a busted heart, for that's how I feel, so home-sick and lonesome that I am really aware of it, turning around in my guts. I guess that it's just that I've been so busy that I haven't had time to really think that much bout home (course I think of you all every day, but you know what I mean), but lately I have been just about to die and this evening I got so homesick I felt like I would throw up.

Me and Patty went downtown today after we got off work at the Hasty Tasty to do some Christmas shopping. There are all kinds of stores up here, you would never get over it in your life. Well, we was down there shopping and we went into this little dress shop and inside they were playing Christmas music real loud. Elvis and Brenda Lee. They even had a loudspeaker outside their shop so you could hear the music when you were looking in the windows.

We were making our way through the dresses, just shopping and cutting up, and all at once, Bill Monroe come over them loud-speakers, singing "Christmas Times A-Coming." I thought I would die stone-hammer dead. There was that high, fine voice amongst all them fiddles and mandolins singing about missing my country home and it made my head swim right back to Free Creek. I couldn't take it, and I left Patty and run outside. But you could still hear the music out there, and I felt like I couldn't run away from it. I leaned against the store window and then slid down it. I am not lying to you. I set down on that cold sidewalk and just let my bags flop over in the snow. I looked up at them tall buildings but all I could picture was the black mountains. I looked at the gray, filthy snow pushed up on the corner and just thought of how back home when it comes a snow in the mornings it would be so smooth and white and sometimes go all day without being traipsed through. There would be just a few little bird tracks, so light and soft that they barely made a print at all. I remembered many a morning when there'd be a snow and I'd throw the back door open and listen to how quiet it was out, and breathe in that good metal taste of cold and smell coal smoke puffing out of every house down the creek. And then Granny would come in and tell me to close the door before I froze every one of us to death. Bill Monroe just kept singing and singing till I thought he'd never hush. I swear to my Lord if I'd had a pistol with me I would have shot that loudspeaker all to Kingdom Come.

Finally Patty come running out to find me and she hunkered down, pulling at my arm to get up. People were stopping to say Is she alright? When Patty finally got me up she said, Honey, what in the hell's the matter with you? and I said to her, I'm so homesick I believe I'm going to die.

We caught the bus straight off and made our way up to Second Street, where our little apartment is, and we went in and there set Simeon drunker than Old Miss Drunk. Eleshia was setting there in the floor playing with her doll and watching the television without him even tending to her. Patty took her hand and knocked his feet off of the coffee table and looked at him like she'd kill him. She said, Our girl's dead to go home now, Simeon, and you've got to take her for Christmas or she'll not make it up here.

Simeon took a slug of whisky right from the bottle and wiped his mouth off on his sleeve and let out a little laugh. Home? he said, and laughed again. You've lost your mind, he said. The Hasty Tasty ain't going to let her off work, and the plant won't let me off, neither. Not for long enough to go to Kentucky.

And I knowed he was right.

Patty told him we were all off two days for the holiday and to take me then but he laughed again. He said it'd take a day to get there and a day to get back, what with the traffic and all. Patty went over to the stove and turned on the ring to light a cigarette. She come back over and put a Lucky in my mouth and hugged me. She told me to come have coffee with her in the morning before work and she left, knowing there was nothing else she could do. Poor old Patty. If it wasn't for her, I'd probably still be setting on that sidewalk. And Bill Monroe would probably still be singing, too.

I just set there. Simeon took another drink of his whisky. He said, Baby I'd like to go home too but we can't afford it, and they ain't no way we can move plumb back, we ain't saved enough money yet.

And that right there done it. We've been up here seven months and ain't a bit better off than when we left Free Creek. We left there with this big dream that we'd come up here and get rich, heard all them tales about people going north like there was some kind of gold rush or something. Just locked the house up and headed out like a couple fools. I told Simeon that, too. He said he wasn't about to work in no coal mines the rest of his life and he wasn't about to come home from work to see me chopping up firewood in the backyard. Then I felt some of my energy come back to me and I throwed a conniption fit. I told him if he didn't pack every rag we had and load it up within two days, then I was catching the train and would send you all a Western Union to pick me up at the depot in Manchester. I told him I couldn't stand it away from home no longer and that was all there was to it. I went to my room and slammed the door.

So here I set, writing this letter.

Oh, Louise, I would give anything in this world to see you. I am thinking of how I used to brush your long, pretty hair every night before you laid down. You would sing to me — Sweet William died for me today, I'll die for him tomorrow. I am looking back to the way Wanda and me would get out in Daddy's truck and go honkytonking (remember that time we wrecked it?), or climb the mountain to see the river sparkling down below. And what I wouldn't do to be able to climb up onto Granny's lap and put my face into the nape of her warm neck! I know this sounds like foolish talk coming from a big twenty-four-year-old girl, but I miss you all so very bad.

I know I am rattling on and on, but I have to go on writing to keep from crying. Simeon still hasn't come in and said to pack my stuff, that we are going home, and he won't neither. I know him better than anybody in this whole world and he is too stubborn to leave without coming home better off. He is drinking more and more since we got up here. There's a bar called Little Mickey's right down the street from our apartment and he stays down there all the time, always telling them factory men about the mines and moonshine. People up here are crazy about those stories and he just adds to things, just feeds them whatever they want to hear. He's sick for home, too. I know he's not happy here neither, but he'd die before he'd admit it.

I hope I beat this letter home. I'm telling you right now, expect something behind this one saying that I am Free Creek bound, because I can't stand much more here, and I know I will never make it through Christmastime if we are here. This ain't an altogether bad place — there is good folks here just like anywhere else — but it's not home, and you know that it is right in our blood to love our land better than anything in this world. And besides, you all are not here.

Anyway, watch for me coming up the road soon with a smile so big that it will blind everybody. I love and miss you all. Remember our good times and when you pray, pray for me. I remain forever

Your loving sister,
Thelma Jean Smallwood

What Child Is This?

by Doris Betts

Her two names—Patty Bell—were always run together and pronounced as one word, Pattybell, emphasis on *Pat,* but attaching the surname for due respect because the Bell family had once been civic leaders in this town. People were glad that her forebears had not survived to witness the condition of this last leaf left on the family tree.

Pattybell was not a mental case, though known to be peculiar. And she was not retarded, only forgetful. Yet her intelligence responded unevenly to life in West Chatham, North Carolina.

Her memory, like a cheap clock, ran slow. Decades ago, the town limits had enclosed a second half, an East Chatham four miles out where Bell Sheeting Mill had stood; now if Pattybell visited its site she seemed astonished that the factory's large brick shell and grounds had been turned into a county park and that fishermen now paddled the reservoir whose dam had once rotated turbines for the plant. Mouth open, she would stand by her classic yellow Mustang (the one many coveted) trying to comprehend the scene: fishermen drifting on the lake above, amateur kayakers riding the river below, and local crafts for sale indoors—nobody any longer making cloth.

Puzzled, she might wander half an hour among picnickers before enough pressure built up to generate her own brain power, then she'd gradually remember how much time had passed since Bell's Mill had closed, because Daddy was dead and foreigners worked cheap. Pattybell would pat her frizzy gray hair, the touch itself reminding her that she'd worn a straw hat on the spring day she'd formally cut the ribbon to dedicate Bell's Mill Park.

On that dedication day she must have been in her late sixties—and now? Eighty? The age of skinny old women is hard to estimate. Once menopause had mummified her, Pattybell stayed just the same.

Since the old Bell house was only half a block from their church, West Chatham's Methodist women unofficially oversaw Pattybell in a benevolent way, though she had not darkened a church door since the day she came home from New York City, having been obscurely ruined up there.

"It was before my time," Mrs. Warlick would tell curious newcomers, "but has been told and *re*told. Pattybell got off the train in Sanford, nobody to meet her, nighttime and the Silver Star going right on down to Florida. Nobody in the railroad station. Not a soul out on the street. She had all her clothes in a sack and I mean a cloth sack like flour used to come in. Well, people say sack but, to be fair, it could've been a laundry bag. At least she had the good sense to walk to the police station, which wasn't far, and ask the policeman on duty to ride her the twenty miles up to West Chatham. Why? Because she was a Bell, she told him. He's supposed to have said that the South might be full of belles but that didn't mean he'd taxi them around. That's too smart a remark, though; I never knew any Sanford policeman bright enough to think up a thing like that."

"So what happened?"

"Of course the man took her, just left the station empty. I can believe that part, all right. She sat in the criminals' backseat and cried all the way home to that empty old house. Every Bell dead but Pattybell. He broke out a back door pane to let her in. No water, no electricity, but it was August so no need for heat."

Sometimes her listeners murmured here or inserted questions.

"Pattybell was studying art up there and living with lesbians at a time nobody here had even learned the word. She's never been the same."

"So before New York she was just fine? As a young girl?"

"I really couldn't say. This was about 1950. I hear she was carried out of some Greenwich Village loft on a stretcher." Mrs. Warlick achieved a dramatic silence by averting her face from this mental image and, after a pause, adding, "Then she was in some institution for a while."

"Does Miss Bell still paint?"

"It was all sculpture, I believe. Here at home she'd do a lamb now and then for some baby's grave, before she got arthritis in both hands."

Pattybell's hands were famous in West Chatham, usually soaked in smelly heating liniments, pushed inside surgical gloves with her fat heirloom rings worn on the outside. Occasionally, while shopping, she squeezed two rubber balls for exercise, and somebody had to chase the one she dropped.

She didn't weigh a hundred pounds, fed herself mostly on fruits, vegetables, and grains—a diet promoted nightly on shortwave by a mellifluous nutritionist who also sold magnets and gold bars and urged his listening audience to write Congress against fluoridation, electric towers, and all child vaccinations.

When Olivia and Curtis Dudley came to tour the brick cottage for sale beside Pattybell's three-story house just down the street from the Methodist spire and belfry, the realtor had not decided how much candor ethics required of him—a *Presbyterian.*

"An old maid," he told the Dudleys with a dismissive wave at the Bell house, whose size magnified its grand disrepair. He added, "Harmless. Pattybell's the town character."

He did not tell the Dudleys that whenever Pattybell pushed her stolen grocery cart uptown, pedestrians could be seen a block or so ahead, fleeing across the street to avoid being trapped to chase balls or hear her talk. They fled her like herds of edible prey in advance of the lion.

Nor did he mention that Pattybell sometimes wandered the neighborhood on nights when she had been chased outdoors by ghosts of former Bells, their spirits stirred up by news of free trade in overseas textiles.

What he *did* say (and this was true, and safer) was that the small bronze stallion that reared upright on a rock in the courthouse annex had been cast by Pattybell many years back. But he decided to omit her marble Greek muse that stood behind a large globe in the library's adult reserve reading room where adolescent boys could not pinch its cold nipples.

To the Dudleys, he pointed out the black iron fence around Pattybell's overgrown acres, shipped from Charleston decades ago, its spear-pointed pickets the work of low-country slaves. He meant them to believe that this fence would enclose her. He did not mention that Pattybell's back lot crossed into another block and then extended past the city limits and that in her own mind there were still two thousand fertile acres stretching beyond that.

"I expect when Pattybell passes on, the old Bell house will be a prime site for the West Chatham Historical Association."

Olivia, too new in town, too new even to the South, didn't care. Her questions were pragmatic: what kind of doctors lived here, how was city trash recycled, who inspected the water supply?

She said to her husband, "I'm not sure about that furnace. You know what a silent killer carbon monoxide can be. And there's not enough space if we ever need a nursery."

The realtor thought she blushed, but he was mistaken.

"Plenty of time," murmured Curtis, a Virginian, who felt northerners like Olivia would expose their private affairs to just anybody.

On cue the realtor indicated how a screened side porch could be closed in, an attic renovated.

"Two fireplaces," Curtis offered.

"And an excellent roof." The realtor fanned the pages of a recent inspection report. "No leaks in the basement. That gas furnace" (he gave Olivia a confident nod) "is only a year old."

Standing at the kitchen sink, Olivia frowned across the black fencing into Pattybell's back yard. "What *is* all that?"

It was a rabbit hutch for one thing — not for a tame white bunny but a wild one she'd trapped and *then* tamed. It was also an odd bird-feeding tower welded onto a metal windmill frame, with catty-cornered hubcaps attached for either seed or fruit eaters, wire holders containing suet, and on its south side a stack of roosting boxes for bad-weather use. No bird that could spend winter nights inside the Methodist belfry or push aside English sparrows to sleep behind the giant warm letters that spelled FOOD LION would condescend to use these boxes, but swarms of birds did eat year-round at Pattybell's. Were eating this very minute while Olivia watched, so many that underneath their cumulative dung the grass had given up.

Pattybell's yard was bordered with vegetable plants instead of flowers, and behind these beds, vines had run up the iron rails and tied gates to their gateposts. Evidently Pattybell liked clematis and bittersweet and Heavenly Blue morning glory and trumpet creeper and ivy and Virginia creeper, all of which, having finished with the fence, then scrambled onto walls and outbuildings that dated back to when this crowded plot had centered the curtilage in a vast Bell farm. Their tenant farmers had grown cotton until the boll weevil came, then tobacco. What land was left now grew broom sedge and red cedars.

Sometimes Pattybell's ivy intruded on the sidewalk, ate the curb, flung its green self downhill in the gutter toward the nutritious sewer. On his own initiative, the city manager sent workers to cut these tendrils back. One year the two-man public works department even sprayed with herbicide. This action sent Pattybell straight to call her shortwave dietician, who telephoned the city offices from someplace in Wyoming and in a cowboy accent threatened West Chatham with lawyers. The resulting controversy got Pattybell nominated for an obscure environmentalist award that during a thin news week brought a TV helicopter from Raleigh to land on the school softball field. For some reason, the interview with Pattybell was never aired.

Such memories composed part of the great clot in the realtor's throat that prevented all he might have told Olivia and Curtis Dudley.

After all, was he the Chamber of Commerce?

No, they closed on the house just as Pattybell's leaves were blowing through and over the wrought iron pickets to blanket their yard, fill their roof gutters and driveway, and even settle in the rusty coal chute Curtis Dudley thought he had closed.

By HALLOWEEN IT was said in West Chatham that the Dudleys were not really settling in. Curtis seemed nice enough, used the local barber and gas station despite making a daily commute to a telecom office twenty miles away. But Olivia, even when seen in the post office or dry cleaners, seemed standoffish, having probably grown up in a tall building with a doorman, where even on elevators nobody said good morning.

The Methodist women understood, even approved, when Olivia visited West Chatham churches before making a choice, but A.M.E. Zion? And then they joined none?

Olivia had also popped up from nowhere in meetings of both the town board and the county commissioners, taking notes, while everyone waited nervously for her to bring up her complaint. When asked, she finally said she was only "taking an interest." To Mrs. Warlick, who in a roundabout way had mentioned that she noticed how often Mrs. Dudley made regular trips to Chapel Hill, Olivia answered with easy candor that she went to a fertility clinic there.

"All the more reason," Mrs. Warlick added to this information while at Jean's Beauty Shop, "for the Dudleys soon to pick a serious church where she could learn what cured Sarah, Hannah, and Elizabeth."

So FAR THE Dudleys had only seen Pattybell at a distance. She drove the Mustang solely on weekends, very slow, and never if it rained. Most days Olivia heard her grocery cart rattling when she pushed it along the sidewalk. Early on November mornings she would roll it curbside in advance of the town trash truck, so she could rake neighbors' leaf piles into plastic bags, carry them home to empty under a tarpaulin in her backyard. Some days she could be seen out back distributing crumbs and black oil sunflower seeds; she might then wave toward their house as if she could see the Dudleys through the walls.

I wish she *could* see, Olivia thought irritably. Let everybody see! See me taking my temperature every sunrise. Eating these pills. Spilling the baking-powder douche. Bracing my feet up the wall after sex to give every slowpoke sperm the advantage of gravity!

At UNC Hospital clinic with her heels in stirrups and both legs spread wide for the fascination of medical students, Olivia could summon real envy for Pattybell and her Greenwich Village lesbians. The more she needed and could not quite enlist sufficient male help to produce a baby, the less Olivia liked men in general.

After enduring one long pelvic exam by an entire gynecology class, Olivia felt her vagina had been turned wrong-side out, like a sleeve.

She finally met Pattybell on a chilly afternoon when she was trying once more to rake oak leaves off the lawn. Olivia was not used to trees that would release a few leaves, then hold back till these were cleared, then perversely detach a second covering.

Through her iron fence Pattybell called, "Just run over them with the lawn mower; it's good for the grass. And I'll borrow it after you're through, please, because mowers are so expensive when a goat can mow weeds and turn them into something usable." She evidently meant usable manure, not milk, for she pointed to a billy goat that must usually stay chained on the far side of the house but now followed her, collar bell ringing, surrounded by a urine stench so thick it should have been visible, like steam. "But don't burn any leaves because if you haven't started a compost pile yet they can go on mine."

"I have one," Olivia lied, thinking compost was one more odd activity in Dixie. She swayed back from the goat who seemed at risk of getting his head hung between pickets while eating her skirt.

"This is a marble salamander," Patty said. She opened one translucent glove to show a small black-and-white creature, half suffocated under eucalyptus and menthol oils. "A male, I think, and if you'll help me tip over my birdbath we can give him a good winter home." She dragged a gate inward making barely enough room for Olivia to scrape past vines and berries.

"Over here!" Already Pattybell was tipping the cement basin so water fell.

Olivia helped her lift off the bowl, then they toppled the heavy base to reveal underneath a filigree of tunnels and channels in the soil.

"Good, they eat earthworms," Pattybell said, scooping out a hole with what looked like a silver serving spoon. She laid the woozy salamander inside. "Quick now!" And they righted and replaced both birdbath sections. Pattybell turned on a hose to refill the bowl.

There were, Olivia now saw, many green hoses snaking from several upright yard spigots. Mrs. Warlick had said that Pattybell still used a deep well dug many years ago underneath the old house; that was why she'd refused to sign on to West Chatham's water supply. She still had a septic tank that dated back who-knew-how-far, buried below a rose thicket, which had naturally exploded into a thorny mountain, so she had passed up the town's sewer service as well.

"Never been pumped out," Mrs. Warlick had reported sadly. "Never. Not one single time."

After that conversation, Olivia had gone into her new basement to examine every stain on every brick, and smell it.

Now she straightened, massaged her spine, and examined the back of the Bell house—three floors, slate roof, green shutters mostly still in place, a wide screened porch with tubs of pansies on each back step. Beyond the rose thicket stood a row of small buildings extending a whole block to the next West Chatham Street; there they picked up on its other side and ran on downhill. Following her gaze, Pattybell shaded her own eyes and stared in the same direction.

"Were those slave cabins?"

"Maybe long ago, but then livestock. Come see." Pattybell set off down the row in her black tennis shoes, talking in a bright ongoing chirp about something Olivia could not quite decipher, and they peeked into stalls with dried anonymous manure, a pigeon coop, an old mew for hawks, the stinking goat pen, another that contained an uneasy tan bitch with pups.

"I don't use them all," said Pattybell when they had reached the last one, enclosed in clear plastic as a greenhouse. Across the next street and beyond, her meadow and underbrush dropped downhill, unkempt, with her row of additional lean-to shacks strung between small modern houses centered in their small landscaped yards. "The children play in them; one got a black widow spider bite. I'm Pattybell. You bought the Richmond house? Look at this mess of iris, you want some? And here are nandina seedlings if you've got a place for them."

Between these sensible sentences Pattybell might croon away or mumble aside in her private language, never quite facing Olivia but turning her eyes here and there as if to confirm the interest of unseen listeners. Such darting glances were contagious; they made Olivia feel some shape had just edged through and beyond the corner of her own eye and vanished.

That night at dinner, Olivia finished her description of the skinny old woman with her wrinkled face as crazed as a pottery jar, and added, "I like her. Poor old thing. I'm going to read up on sculpture so I can talk art to her. Nobody else here does."

"That's just like you, to make Pattybell your latest research project." Curtis passed his plate for more roast. "And don't be such a snob about West Chatham."

She sliced toward fat and gristle. "You've been telling me to make more friends."

"The town crazy? Did I say cultivate the town crazy?"

They had scheduled sex for tonight so both were tense.

Olivia wondered if women, under stress, might be able to hold back on ovulation no matter what the thermometer promised, just suck in their eggs and dry them into pellets. She said carefully, "Pattybell wants to give us a puppy."

"If you want to take care of one, fine. You're home all day."

Did he mean she was lazy? "I can always go back to teaching, you know. I could start a revolution in West Chatham just by teaching the younger generation to pronounce their consonants. I can—"

His interruption sounded far too patient. "We agreed—the doctors said and we agreed—on an easier schedule for you. No pressure. So go ahead, get the dog. It might help."

Curtis meant "help" in the same way that wives who adopted children then would stop consciously trying too hard, and quickly conceive. By mothering as little as a single dog, even Olivia might rejuvenate her ovaries.

She said through her teeth, "OK, I will."

"Lonnie called me at the office today."

"Alonzo. He asked us to call him Alonzo. How is he?"

"While he's here I'll say Alonzo. Next week. He's coming through on a buying trip. I told him the guest room would be ready by then."

"I guess it'll have to be."

"Don't look at me like that. It's way upstairs and on the back; who needs curtains? He'll be no trouble. If fact, you've always gotten along better with Lonnie than me."

Almost true, she had to admit. Especially just before and right after she and Curtis were married and saw him a lot. His brother Alonzo could talk books, films, music; Curtis preferred sports and military history. Alonzo owned a gift and antique shop from which he gave lovely presents. No curtains? You bet she would have to hang curtains.

Alonzo had lived for years with another man who clerked in that antique shop, though Curtis no longer minded that much and Olivia not at all. Or not until recently. During this eighth year of marriage, she'd begun to question whether the Dudley genes might lack sufficient Y chromosomes, whether Curtis might rank only a few masculine degrees above Alonzo—thus just over the heterosexual line. Perhaps the real job of procreation had (like its former prevention) been delegated to her alone.

Of course, doctors in Chapel Hill, like those back in Providence, kept saying Curtis had a low but probably sufficient sperm count; still, she had observed that men would stick together in matters involving macho pride. When she lay naked in wide-open postures in their sterile examining rooms, men in white coats frowned at her private parts; did they direct such a frown to Curtis? Their long silences seemed to blame her. And why was every speculum stored in a refrigerator? If a sperm count was low, its motility slow, was it really up to Olivia to relocate and expand her own reluctant target? Reduce acidity? Ovulate more often? With greater enthusiasm?

Over congealing beef gravy, she and Curtis had now passed too much time without speaking. Stacking their plates, Olivia said, "I don't want to housebreak a dog while we have company."

Curtis had just been waiting for her to say the wrong thing. He threw up both hands, his napkin a white flag. "So don't then, Olivia, whatever you want! Whatever you don't want!"

She carried their plates to the kitchen, waited an extra minute at the sink to compose herself. In Pattybell's yard the billy goat was chained to a concrete block that he couldn't drag far. The Bell house was dark.

When Olivia returned, she was able to say, "If you help with the dishes" (her smile simultaneously sweet and threatening) "we can go to bed early."

Now the permanent dimple by his mouth gave a twitch. She saw him curb that muscle, knew he had concluded it would be wise to change the subject.

"What kind of dog is it?" he asked.

Ah, but now she was ready. "The mother's a golden retriever, purebred. Nobody knows anything about the father."

FOUR DAYS LATER, as soon as a horn blew shave-and-a-haircut, Olivia ran to the front door and watched Alonzo Dudley lift from his Mercedes a small piece of furniture, mahogany by its color, two-tiered and three-legged, meant to fit neatly into the corner of a tasteful room.

Immediately she knew she had hung curtains of an inferior type and color.

"Housewarming!" Alonzo called, with so high a swoop that it must weigh very little on those straight and slender legs. Olivia had a dim realization that Pattybell and perhaps the goat had drawn close to their side of the fence to see. "It's a wash stand!"

Instantly joyous, she ran down the steps and over the flagstone walk to hug him, to suck in a lungful of that toiletry fragrance Curtis called gay pheromone. Alonzo gripped her inside one tight arm, still lofting his present overhead.

"I'm so glad to see you, so glad, so very glad!" She pressed her face to his Adam's apple. "Oh, I've missed you!"

"Careful, this is early 1800s, made in South Carolina, Sheraton type—you like it?"

"I love it!"

Delicately, Alonzo backed Olivia out of reach and risk, an act that reminded her how much more he valued things over people. Gently he lowered the wash stand to the sidewalk, clapped his hands. "The standard bowl and pitcher go on the top shelf. Hand towels below, I guess. Look at those medallions!"

"We'll put it right in the guest room."

"Close to me? Good, because I can hardly bear to part with this beauty. Only for you, Olivia. Curtis wouldn't care if I brought an orange crate. Lead on. But Olivia, this is a small town, isn't it? Where do you eat out? Where do you see movies?"

"Chapel Hill, Raleigh, Durham."

He said grimly, "But does anybody live here you can talk to?"

Ahead of him she danced backward, enjoying the full sight of his wavy, too-long hair, blond where Curtis was brown, his eyes bright blue while Curtis had a paler, almost gray pair behind his half glasses, and Alonzo with dimples notched into both cheeks instead of one.

Following, Alonzo moved lightly, arms wrapped around the antique. Olivia knew that, should she fall, he would first set down the furniture piece and steady it carefully in place before offering her his hand. It was a comfort, Olivia thought, to know where his emotional edges were. Curtis was less consistent.

"But this seems nice, this house," he was saying almost reluctantly, "and what color will you paint the front door?" Then he placed the wash stand securely on the front porch and shaded his eyes. "Is that person real?"

"That's Pattybell next door. She's the last of the town's founders or something."

"But that iron fence, my God! How far does it go? Do you have any idea—"

"Of what it would cost now, no, I don't. Come on inside, Alonzo, have a drink while I bring in your bag."

When he rolled his eyes it deepened their blue. "So you *can* drink here. I didn't see a single liquor store on the highway."

He would need, Olivia knew from experience, an hour or so before he had used up, worn out, and moved beyond his resident-gay routine, dropped the italics, lowered his flying eyebrows, reduced the hand gestures and grimaces. His performance had never been aimed at Olivia but might express a version of durable sibling rivalry toward Curtis, who was not here now to be suitably annoyed. Back in Providence, when Alonzo had come to join their other dinner guests, such mannerisms had never been wasted on strangers.

From the porch Olivia called, "Pattybell? Come meet my brother-in-law."

Pattybell entered into warfare with the overgrown gate, won, and thrust herself toward them almost shyly, but extended her ungloved hand high as if it had been made for kissing.

Alonzo didn't go that far, perhaps because his own light fragrance had been swept away by the tidal wave of her menthol. Before names could be exchanged, Pattybell rubbed the high curve of the wash stand he had been guarding on Olivia's porch. She said, "I've got one of these."

"Oh, I doubt it," said Alonzo—but politely.

Less polite, Pattybell said, "Two," then to Olivia, "when do you want your pup?"

"Uh, next week? I need to fix him a bed and a place—"

"Fine," said Pattybell, adding to Alonzo, "I've got a sideboard with those legs but three curves in front. I've got a card table but the maple's veneer. And other things." She enjoyed seeing his mouth under the matched blond mustache go slack. "I've got a secretary goes back even before, got an eagle on its top. Has a shield and thirteen stars on its breast."

By now Alonzo had stepped away from Olivia entirely, even deserting the wash stand.

"Look at that ol' goat," said Pattybell. "There's an inlaid eagle on the rolltop but it's just pine except for the panels. Not walnut or anything."

Olivia could see that Alonzo had gone weak in the knees from longing. "I'd love," he breathed out hard, "to see it. Them."

But Pattybell had launched into one of her long confusing harangues about the goat, the rabbit, her father's cigars, the running-wild children who'd thrown raw eggs on her porch on Halloween night, a flock of cedar waxwings that had just this morning stripped her holly bush and flew on.

Olivia understood by now that some of these digressions were involuntary, while others constituted Pattybell's strategic avoidance, as in saving her now from the rudeness of telling Alonzo that visitors were never welcome inside her house.

Still talking, in a part whisper now, Pattybell wandered away to relocate the cement block and the billy goat it anchored.

"You've fallen in with strange locals," Alonzo observed as he followed Olivia down her wide hall, touching the wainscoting as he went, pausing to examine a wall sconce that immediately looked flimsy. Climbing the stairs, he balanced the wash stand overhead. "Would that woman sell anything, you think?"

Olivia thought not.

In the guest room, Alonzo chose straightaway the corner where his gift would be best displayed. Then from the center he pivoted to take in the pale tulips in the wallpaper, matched by pastel curtains. Olivia had whitened the woodwork with bleach, waxed the wide-board floor.

"Very nice," Alonzo said. "But those curtains have got to go."

She nodded quickly. "They came with the house."

He asked if she had lemon oil, not some silicone spray but plain old lemon oil. After Olivia had found a bottle and rag, she left him to get settled and to polish the corner wash stand.

SHE HAD ACTUALLY met Alonzo before Curtis, while doing graduate work in Providence. Without the help of her home parish, Olivia could never have afforded college; their scholarship sent her to the liberal arts Providence College, a Catholic school she might not otherwise have chosen.

Even as early as high school, Olivia had been more than ready to replace her faith in God with faith in science, so it was thus galling to find herself on a Catholic campus as a recipient of Catholic generosity—just as now it was galling to find the reproductive sciences so ineffective.

Back then, she did not trust that faculty to tell her any disturbing truths about evolution, genetics, psychology, nor assign any novels in favor of secularism, much less blasphemy. She had majored in English and history, though one professor wrote on an essay, "Miss Connor, you have taken this poem so deep into the frigid zone of your attention that I doubt it can thaw out in just one semester."

Olivia thought this an unjust criticism of her thoroughness.

Still, she graduated with sufficient high grades to warrant even further subsidy by superstitious believers, who next underwrote postgraduate education courses that would certify her to teach her subjects in secondary schools. She was very good at lesson plans.

She thrived on developing a syllabus, and a full curriculum even more.

Enrolled in that teachers' preparatory program, she was working as part-time guide at Pendleton House when Alonzo Dudley came to tour its rooms of eighteenth- and nineteenth-century furniture.

It had been easy to memorize long narratives about museum holdings, but Olivia was startled when Alonzo broke into her automatic spiel with an impatient, "Oh, do be quiet." Then he violated all regulations by opening drawers and sliding heavy pieces out from the wall and telling her which hand tool had performed which laborious woodworking task and how many man-hours every inlay had taken. Olivia would have been angry had she not heard in his tone a love for the object itself, and respect for what lay behind appearances. It was as if Alonzo could still see the ghostly hands of artisans now dead, or know how each scratch and scar formed an abbreviation of family stories. (She had since learned how much he preferred most human beings at a remove—of time, of distance.)

That day he took Olivia to lunch—good, her funds were low.

Over wine (at noon!) Olivia wondered silently what life would be like for a woman who fell in love with, chose even to marry, a man who did not desire her at all but preferred other men— Alonzo had been very candid very early. In those days she was still a virgin (another problem the Catholics had caused), and while she watched Alonzo talking, laughing, running a fingertip along his mustache to cherish its texture, Olivia could even picture the two of them: in Technicolor, reading aloud poetry by firelight. Later, they would lie lovingly but chastely in each others arms and talk. They would both have British accents.

Over their large salads (for Alonzo did not then or now eat murdered cows or pigs) Olivia visualized them in historical, heavily curtained beds, both clad in embroidered and unrevealing nightshirts, propped high and neutral on fat silken pillows. Talking. *Talking!*

If Alonzo was a wonderful lunchtime talker, he was an even better listener. Now, nine years later, Olivia could still remember how easily his wide-eyed interest had seen past her own surface, as if her real self—like furniture—had been obscured under shellac and varnish and paint. By instinct he probed to her fear of going unmarried and unfucked to her grave, unused by life (whatever that meant). Untried. With a steady gaze he traveled the strata of her psyche: a shiny surface of scientific method and schoolteacher habit laid above nun, bluestocking, vulnerable spinster, terrified old crone.

Hindsight, of course. All Olivia had known then, nearly nine years before, was her own rushing emotional release from admitting so much. If asked, she would have confidences equal on both sides— two childhoods, four parents, multiple longings. She never noticed when the talk shifted from their dialogue to her confessional.

"But I'm a very competent teacher!" she insisted several times. Not talented. Not passionate. Certainly not beloved.

Today, Olivia remembered this first and their subsequent lunches as oral exams she was passing without knowing, tests that had qualified her as suitable for Curtis, who was then a graduate student in computer science at Brown and, in Alonzo's opinion, not self-assertive enough.

Slowly, Alonzo aligned them, drew them toward each other, the way a fisherman who is convinced that two prime specimens have been safely contained will lift the wide net here, and then there, sliding them closer to each other. For weeks he tantalized each one with anecdotes about the other, samples of how similar or compatible they were, predictions of what good friends they would become.

Then? A luxury threesome lunch at a big hotel, Alonzo's treat.

An arranged telephone message that called him away.

Olivia had been left with sour lettuce she had not wanted but had ordered in case both brothers were vegetarians, left with the younger Curtis: same tousled hair, no mustache, paler eyes — perhaps paler altogether — a dry, deprecating wit, expert in a discipline she understood as well as Zulu.

By the time they were eating sorbet, Olivia did understand, though could not verbalize, that platonic love did leave off where sex began. It was obvious that if her library card had been laid beside Curtis Dudley's, not a single title would match. And yet, as if stroked by feathers or sable brushes, whole sections of her skin began to prickle, when not a single goosebump had been summoned by Alonzo. She squirmed in her chair, enjoyed the squirming.

When their fingers touched on the sugar bowl, her hand flared warm to the wrist. And from low in her stomach rose a puzzling sensation that mixed pleasure with near nausea. She crossed her legs tightly.

Such unexpected behavior by her body had at the time persuaded Olivia that, though she'd lost faith in God, she still believed that for every woman there was one "right man," that happy couples were those who had always been "meant for each other," body mates more than soul mates, and that though only a metaphor, a marriage "made in Heaven" was a *true* metaphor.

Remembering that lunch, recalling its sudden sexual undercurrent, Olivia now felt her mouth lift by itself in the start of smiling, the resurgence of hope.

Then Alonzo called from upstairs, "What in the hell is a luna kit?"

He must have found hers in the bathroom. "It tests my saliva," she called back. "Most days I get little dots. But on fertile days my spit will turn into, well, a fern."

"You're kidding, right?"

"It crystallizes in the shape of ferns."

She heard Alonzo mutter, then close a bathroom drawer on her record of dots and lines and occasional lacy fronds.

But he had made her think, for the first time, of something one doctor had suggested and she had back then set aside: that some husbands eventually became willing to thicken their own sperm with ejaculate obtained from a kinsman, keeping the genes similar, any infant's resemblance convincing. When a baby was born with the family chin or nose, a husband would usually believe himself the actual father.

As if transfixed, Olivia stood in the downstairs hall while above her the toilet flushed and fluid poured behind plaster through the pipes and drained away.

He'd never agree to do it, never; of course, she knew that—and decided immediately that tonight she'd approach Curtis. Ask him. Beg.

MELLOWED BY ALONZO's wine the three of them enjoyed an easy, laughing time at dinner and afterward, touring the house and peering through upstairs windows to see into Pattybell's in search of priceless antiques. Since he had no binoculars and the long drive had tired him, Alonzo went to bed early. From the bathroom door he asked, "You need your fern box?"

"No," but she did retrieve her pill bottle. Alonzo got on the upstairs phone to check in with his partner, Edward, sounding very domestic.

In their bedroom Olivia put on a blue lace nightgown, tried to call back that long ago lunch, those used-to-be sensations. But it was a dot night, not a fern night, and nowadays she almost hated to waste sex on nothing but pleasure.

Curtis, down to his underwear and as much aware as she that the fertility chart was low tonight, raised both eyebrows and waited. He had lost weight, Olivia thought, so parts of him had sharpened since their move to West Chatham, not just the knees and elbows, but his chin, his wrist bones; even the knob in his throat seemed angular. Sometimes he spoke with sympathy of stallions and dogs whose main occupation was standing at stud. He had made such remarks lightly at first; lately the words contained vinegar. Once he had rolled off her body with a mumble about probably "shooting blanks," a metaphor she hated.

Before he could stop her now or Olivia could stop herself, she plunged rapidly into her proposal, well—no, the doctor's proposal, really—about using fraternal sperm. Immediately, his thinner face congested red and he began slapping the air. "No, absolutely not, no way!" He was so loud that perhaps Alonzo could hear him through the walls. "How could you even think such a thing? You must be crazy. It's driven you crazy. It's driving me crazy! Not another word, Olivia!" He pushed empty space away from himself, a current to sweep through the air anything more she might say. "Crazy even to consider it! My God!"

Probably he would have left the room had she not backed against the door. "Why not? Calm down, Curtis. Apart from your pride, just give me one reason why not?"

"That's long gone, pride."

The way his upper lip got flat and stiff, as when a boy instructs himself that he's way too old to cry, made Olivia put her arms around him, though he stood within her warmth like a post.

She said softly, "The doctor says mixing them only raises the chance of success. You'd still be—"

"I know what I'd be." He stepped away. Yes, his ribs were showing. "We long ago agreed that Alonzo was born his way—right? It's all genes, not just a lifestyle choice. So you want to raise a little fag or a dyke of our own?"

"Curtis Dudley!"

He threw himself onto the bed, crawled across to his side and lay facing away. "Don't ever mention this to me again, Olivia. I mean it."

Through gritted teeth she said, "Fine." And again, "Fine." She hit the light switch with the heel of her hand and eased onto as narrow a mattress space as possible. She could hear both of them faking the deep breaths that would lead to sleep, though their bodies were too tight, all muscles far too tight. Both were now stiffened into posts, hard wooden posts that used to be alive.

Next morning Curtis left without waking her. No breakfast, so for Alonzo alone she cooked southern food guaranteed to clog arteries: eggs with country ham and grits and the redeye gravy she'd learned from Pattybell, its center darkened by a little coffee. Because she insisted that he try the local delicacies, Alonzo temporarily forfeited his vegetarianism, but after overdramatized chewing, he pushed the meat aside, saying that country ham should always be served with a side order of dental floss. "Although this morning you look more in need of Kleenex. Is it a problem, Olivia? Having me visit?"

She shook her head and sniffed once. "Next time I'll try biscuits."

In truth, she was not much of a cook. She liked no-fail recipes, like chemical formulae. She hated to estimate dashes and pinches, or to follow advice like "season to taste."

"Nothing wrong between you and Curtis?"

"Just the usual."

"I've already told you both—adopt! You can just about order European babies on the Internet!" He studied her failure to smile, then gave a slight shudder. "I hope you're not taking those medicines that make women drop a whole litter at once."

"I don't want to talk about it, I'm sick of the subject."

"Curtis, too, I expect." When she nodded Alonzo pushed back his plate. "So you're going to show me the town?" She said the whole tour would take maybe five minutes but he interrupted. "Invite Miss Pattybell. She must know the local history. And I'm going to charm her, you'll see, so she'll show me what treasures are inside her house." At Olivia's frown he added quickly, "I'd never cheat her, dear, fair price and all that."

"Nobody ever goes inside her house. Some boy tried a front window on Halloween night and he got a face full of floor mop. Ammonia. His mother thought he had conjunctivitis—pinkeye they call it here."

But Alonzo planned to be invited in through the front door, as Olivia could tell when she was relegated to his backseat and a flustered Pattybell sat beside him in the Mercedes. Today she was wearing a dark green coat with a collar of fur so unpleasant in feel and color that it might have come from the goat, and she'd drawn a streak of pink across her thin upper lip only.

"And around the courthouse circle," she directed Alonzo. "Do it again. Did you know one day a man just kept going around and around until finally a secretary noticed it out her office window? He'd had a stroke or something. Go east now."

She had seldom heard Pattybell speak so clearly or well. Perhaps all she really needed was personal attention. Olivia felt vaguely jealous.

"Church, of course, not much to see there."

"I went there a Sunday or so."

"You, Olivia?" Alonzo laughed. "Bible Belt getting to you?"

Olivia leaned over the seat back. "Did you make the lamb on that gravestone? Or the angel?"

Nervously, Pattybell said she didn't remember. When she waved her gloved hand out the window, the pungent smell that blew off seemed to dampen Olivia's face.

In front Pattybell was making a rapid list of buildings they passed. "Sears. Family Dollar. Kerr Drug. Food Tiger. Lion? Domino's Pizza. Then nothing but houses until the river bridge."

They were going, Olivia realized, to Bell's Mill Park, in now defunct East Chatham where the few remaining mill houses had in recent years been rented by students from Chapel Hill who planted marijuana in former garden plots—its brilliant green vegetation usually spotted by the state helicopter.

"Close the window," Olivia said, growing uneasy without cause. Pattybell was so excited at being tour guide for the day that some misuse of her innocence seemed likely to occur. Olivia listened to Alonzo charm her with respectful questions and comments, though the details she gave him — such as who had once owned that field or those woods — were boring.

"You'll wear her out," Olivia heard herself say protectively. He did not answer.

Theirs was one of only several cars parked by the muddy river and the almost as muddy lake, and they were among a small number of other customers who were shopping the craft stalls for late Christmas gifts. On the highly varnished pine floors, their footsteps echoed in the huge rooms. From display booths came occasional calls of "Hey, Pattybell," toward which she waved her gloved hand. She passed by quilts and baskets, talking nonstop to Alonzo.

"To begin with the Bells had a grist mill on the river, and then after the Civil War they started this factory to make sheeting and yarn. I think the spindles were in this big room here, Ring warp spindles. Papa brought home spools and things for us to play with."

"Us?" Olivia's voice was almost a croak. "Us?"

"I had a sister." She moved ahead of them both, bent but fast, and Alonzo gave a shrug before following.

Staring out one of the tall, glazed windows, Pattybell absently removed a tennis ball from the dreadful coat and squeezed it, sending a pulsation of odors into surrounding air.

Olivia drew closer through the cloud. "Your sister. Is she — ?"

"Oh, certainly. She was older." Pattybell stepped to another window, through which the lake could only be seen as a shimmer. "Drowned right there."

"Your sister drowned right here? When was this? What happened?"

"And I went to New York," said Pattybell. She flexed the tennis ball once more before putting it away and leading them outdoors. She had apparently lost interest in the room or what remained of the old mill, though outdoors Olivia and Alonzo gaped at bare empty walls that were still attached to the crafts room and jutted from its corners, walls with no roof, enclosing only cracked but cleanly swept concrete floor that had picnic tables scattered about.

"It burned?" Alonzo guessed and Olivia nodded. Great chunks of masonry, especially from the collapsed three-story tower, had been hauled to one side, covered with topsoil and seeded with grass, and turned into child-sized mountains where an annual Easter egg hunt was held.

Alonzo caught up with Pattybell and expressed an interest in seeing some of her artwork.

She nodded and led the way to the car, talking rapidly to herself, and at her direction they drove to a community called Merry Oaks and in it the Christian Chapel Christian Church—too many redundancies for Olivia—where Pattybell showed them a cherub resting atop a child's tombstone. It was white stone, and pockmarked; some vandal had painted red toenails on the chubby feet. Otherwise the statuary was a standard graveyard cliché. They moved awkwardly around to examine every side. Nobody had anything to say.

"Time to go home," Pattybell announced with sudden cheer, and that was the end of the grand tour. On the drive back, she held one arm straight out the window, as a child might, practicing the scythe gesture that mentally sliced off trees and decapitated chimneys.

The reality of that game was confirmed for Olivia when Pattybell said, as she climbed out of Alonzo's car, "I heard once about a man whose wife died and he was so grief stricken that he sawed off every tree around his house about five feet high, and he carved her there. Over and over."

She waved at them and was gone.

ON THE NIGHT before Alonzo left, Olivia lay sleepless beside a restive Curtis, who seemed to be dreaming something about a zoo. Sometimes he gave off a growl.

She went on bare feet to the bathroom. The small night bulb gave only a knee-high glow, as if she were wading in light. She sat on the toilet, could not urinate, moved past the mirror and stepped into the tub to look at Pattybell's house through the small, high window. By now she knew there had never been a sister for Pattybell, must have been—said Mrs. Warlick—"one of those imaginary playmates." She knew also that soon after sunrise, Pattybell would be coming down those back steps with her night jar, in which her own overnight urine—thinned with water—would be applied to the roots of some runaway bush.

Olivia, feeling lax and dreamy, allowed herself to slump, to bend, and then to surprise herself by lying down flat inside the cold tub.

She lay very still, bone against porcelain, feeling like a dead person.

For awhile there were no thoughts in her head. This house that would always be called the Richmond and never the Dudley house gave off a creak and tick. Her hip and shoulder blades began to ache. All the young Richmonds lived in Charlotte now. It was said that someday they'd probably appear and ask to see what she'd done with their house. It was assumed that she'd be happy to show them every neat nook and cranny.

She crawled out, clumsily.

I could go out that door and turn left down the hall instead of right. I could show Alonzo what to do, just as a favor to me. A favor to us. He wouldn't have to like it. Neither one of us would like it, and that's as it should be.

Olivia tiptoed back to her own bed, ashamed.

DURING THE FIRST nights, the pup whined for its mother and littermates. In a cardboard box by their bed, he disproved any theory that a ticking clock could replace a canine heartbeat, though sometimes Olivia's hand, if dangled down, would soothe him, perhaps by its warm pulse. Curtis slept through all this.

The puppy's fur was tan, eyes golden brown, and the hairs on the edge of both ears grew slightly curled. His chest was bibbed in white. His small round puddles of pee appeared everywhere. It infuriated Olivia to see Curtis step over these and walk on by. Not likely to turn into a hands-on father, Olivia thought.

But it was Curtis's grumble that the dog must have a kidney the size of Texas that settled the name, usually reduced to Tex, and sometimes said in a groan as Olivia rushed forward with another paper towel.

Pattybell had found homes for the other five pups by a simple stratagem: she wheeled the boxload in her grocery cart to the Food Lion parking lot where she posted a sign, FREE PUPPIES. For perhaps an hour she beckoned to every passing child.

Afterward, Olivia drove her to the vet to have the bitch spayed, for a fee so low that she wondered if all of West Chatham gave discounts to Pattybell, the way old-time grocers handed out peppermints.

The next week it seemed a logical trade-off for Pattybell to ride along to Chapel Hill and sit in the clinic's waiting room while Olivia reported another month's failure. She had to smile watching other patients slide their glances sideways, while they guessed that Pattybell might be a grandmother with handicaps. It was the other way 'round. Olivia took on years and maturity when they were together.

Later, riding the open-air shuttle to and from the hospital parking lot, Pattybell laughed aloud. She behaved as if this vehicle were a carnival ride, gripping the rail while opening her dentures wide to the cold wind. Her obvious enjoyment made Olivia ask, "How long has it been, Pattybell, since you went anywhere outside West

Chatham?" But Pattybell, instead of answering, went on waving at riders on other shuttle vehicles.

After she had paid the parking fee and driven into the weak winter sunlight, Olivia asked what they might do next. "Christmas shopping? I'm done with mine but we could certainly."

Pattybell shook her head.

"I got Alonzo some really beautiful cuff links. You know he'd love to buy any antique furniture you might someday want to sell?" While talking on one subject, Olivia was wondering about others: Pattybell's income, her health insurance. Her health, period. "Will you be staying home over Christmas?"

"If not, who would look after my animals?"

"Why I, I suppose I could actually feed the goat and the rabbit. The dog," said Olivia slowly. "Your birds."

With one glove, Pattybell lightly rubbed her knuckles along Olivia's cheek. Then she announced that she was hungry.

Olivia chose a drive-through window for hamburgers and fries they could eat in the car. She no longer wanted others to stare at the unlikely pair they made and speculate. "Here's another napkin!" she cried as red ketchup dripped onto upholstery.

"Don't need it," said Pattybell. When she chewed with her mouth open something clicked in her mouth, false teeth or perhaps the joints in her jaw.

On the way home, soon after she finished eating, Pattybell fell asleep with her forehead resting against the passenger window, sending a shiver across her steel-wool hair.

So Olivia and Curtis invited Pattybell for dinner on Christmas Eve. Olivia spent the day roasting a turkey so large that she doubted its inner core could ever be cooked enough to be safe from salmonella. She burned her arm during many deep thrusts of the meat thermometer.

"You'd think the woman was royalty, all this trouble," said Curtis as with one shoe he slid Tex farther from the hot and aromatic oven.

Olivia turned toward the kitchen window with its view of the iron fence, stark and black now under twisted dead twigs. She did not want him to see how close she was to tears. Tears for no reason at all! Ever since her last checkup she had felt jumpy, depressed. Something kept enlarging itself, but in the wrong place—her throat. There seemed no new cause since she was still not pregnant. Perhaps she was reeling under the onslaught of Christmas itself. Radio and television were drowning her in carols, jingle bells, Santa ho-hos. Her eyeballs crackled from so much premature tinsel, so many blinking lights. Unlike Providence, West Chatham was relentless in Christian observance of the holiday. Though only a few stores lined the two downtown streets and most people drove to city malls, every local shop had displayed a crèche in the window or a huge Madonna portrait painted in too many primary colors. Three downtown churches competed in living manger scenes on their front lawns. Since the Methodists had live sheep and one bawling cow in theirs, long lines of cars drove slowly past the Dudley house to see. Some parked in their drive so the children could walk closer. People the Dudleys did not know or could not remember meeting sent Christmas cards with local postmarks, cards that featured wise men, shepherds, and the babe. Even the postman, their newspaper boy, and the realtor who had sold them the house and never been seen again, mailed them cards. On their same block, neighbors had propped lighted Santas as well as angels on their front porch roofs, the angels in a two-to-one ratio. And from December 1 on, after every sunset there floated above the unused courthouse chimney a mammoth spangled star tethered on a long cord to the old brickwork so every wind would shift it to and fro and cause wandering mottled light to cross and recross the bronze Confederate soldier who posed below, facing up the main street and north forever.

Where, Olivia had wondered aloud to Curtis, were West Chatham's atheists and Jews?

Pattybell loved the season, too, and made them a wreath that seemed to be based on honeysuckle.

Now, and although she kept her face turned away, Curtis drew Olivia close. "Something wrong?"

"I don't know why I'm so jittery. I do hate to cook but—" (she let out a little scream). The back door had opened suddenly and banged the refrigerator. Pattybell stepped in, smiling. Tonight she seemed to have reddened only her lower lip, but she also wore long pearl earrings, which dragged down her limp earlobes. She held out a plate of deviled eggs, which, she said, "Mrs. Warlick brought. She brought a whole basket of stuff. I hate fruitcake, don't you?"

With a broad smile Curtis said, "Merry Christmas." Perhaps he was just trying not to laugh when Pattybell halfway tripped on her long black skirt, whose velvet was sun-streaked in long, pale stripes. He was standing too far away to perceive, as Olivia did, that Pattybell had managed to tweezer off the occasional white hairs usually growing at or just underneath her chin and wrapped her head in a scarf so she had flowers growing there instead of hair. These efforts touched her, so she gave Pattybell an impulsive hug that sent one egg-half off the plate onto the floor. Tex swallowed it whole.

It turned out that, for ease of transport, Pattybell had suspended two bottles of wine around her thin waist from a belt of clothesline. With theatrical swoops she presented, first, the homemade scuppernong, then the other—a dry white Bordeaux marked 1937. Olivia thought this was probably one of many bottles lying dusty but mellow in the drawers and cubbies of antique Bell furniture.

When he read the label Curtis said, "Good Lord." He set the wine on a counter and with some gallantry got Pattybell eased into a chair. "We'll have that at dinner but meantime you'll join us" (he poured malt scotch over one ice cube in a small glass) "in wishes not just for Christmas but the New Year. New beginnings. New hopes."

Was he winking at her? He could already be, thought Olivia, just a little drunk. "You two move to the living room while I finish up here. Maybe fifteen more minutes," she added, though how on earth real cooks could estimate she'd never known.

Like an insistent Boy Scout, Curtis was guiding the woman by her elbow. She came nowhere near his shoulder.

Olivia stirred gravy, then checked the rice in the steamer. She could hear their voices murmur, low and high, low and high, equal amounts of talk and answer. Really, when he wanted, Curtis could be very fair, very kind! He was letting Pattybell talk the most. It roused in her that tender affection that sometimes would ripen into desire, a reverse of how for Curtis sex always came first, embraces afterward.

Olivia pressed the apron to her flat stomach, hoping for daughters.

What could they be finding to talk about? The Christmas tree? Some ornaments had come from the Dudley house when those in-laws died; this year she had even hung the New Testament ones from home. In the middle of a sparse angelic host she had set a Santa who wore an expression like King Herod in disguise.

Curtis might be showing off his new gas logs, making the flame go red to blue. Pattybell might respond with anything at all, was just as apt to show him the magnets wrapped in elastic around one knee or to volunteer details about her missing sister who was sometimes Velma and sometimes Imogene but always dead.

Olivia checked the dining room table with its centerpiece of holly and cedar. She hoped Curtis had not already shown Pattybell the package with her name on it.

But when she carried in a small plate of cheese and crackers the big golden box was resting on Pattybell's velvet lap, and Pattybell was almost paralyzed with pleasure. She touched the red ribbon, drew back. She slid the box from side to side across her thighs.

"I have not!" Pattybell was breathing fast. "In so long I never. Nobody did."

"Ah, Pattybell!" Olivia pushed the plate of snacks into view, almost ashamed that she had chosen, first, a silk scarf she had not been able to visualize around Pattybell's neck until seeing tonight's hair wrap, so had added a hobby set for making figurines. Surely Pattybell would be mystified by the first gift, insulted by the second.

Curtis sprang into the awkward moment. "Did you put up a Christmas tree, Pattybell?"

She shook her head. She kept holding onto her present with both hands.

Olivia said she was going to close the puppy into an upstairs room so they could eat in peace.

Tex had to be carried to their room—God forbid that he should ever whet those sharp puppy teeth on Alonzo's night stand! His belly was distended from food and in a few minutes he spread out to sleep. Olivia watched, thinking the dog was turning out to be, as Curtis had predicted, therapeutic. His scrambling on a slick floor made her laugh. They had already been to the veterinarian for worming, shots, since Pattybell believed in neither.

Olivia laid her fingers between the pup's stubby front legs, to feel the fast thrumming of the small heart, then touched her own nose to revisit the smell of new fur, young skin.

If she had not been kneeling at the dog's basket under the window, it would have been much later before anyone saw the growing light next door. Olivia frowned. Did Pattybell have a Christmas tree after all?

Then she screamed, "Fire!" and kept on screaming as she bolted out the door, clattered down the stairs, burst into the room with one hand thrown forward to Pattybell, yelling, "You! Yours!" and running past them to the telephone.

ALL CHRISTMAS EVE night the Bell house burned. Some said the mill had smoldered for a week, but few of those spectators were still alive to make comparisons.

Tonight's spectators, though, came to park in the churchyard and walk as close as firemen allowed. Yet they were careful to step with precision through the Methodist cemetery without putting one shoe on one grave. The temporary pine-slab stable shook when people bumped against its walls, but nobody touched the manger or the baby doll inside.

Pattybell's billy goat ran wild in the street. Cats leapt from her windows. Somebody rescued the rabbit cage and set it atop Curtis's car.

There was nothing to be done. Olivia held Pattybell back from her instinctive rush toward home, finally forced her to sit on the Dudleys' porch steps by bending those knees, magnets and all, and pressing those bony shoulders down. Flakes of ash came by them, or touched their skin.

Later, the fire chief would say the cause was probably electrical. Old wiring, he said, and spread his hands as if the frayed wires ran from thumb to thumb. Mice. All that accumulated dust and spiderwebs. Tinderbox.

Pattybell looked straight through him and into the blaze.

She did not cry or, if she did, the waves of heat that blew against them dried and reddened her face.

The firemen were dousing those trees that might catch fire either at the Dudleys or the brick house on the other side. West Chatham's two trucks had been joined by volunteer firemen from out in the county and beyond. Their arcs of water played over the space where the third floor had already dropped, and through these silvery movements sparks flew up to the stars. Two of the plastic displays of Peace-on-Earth candles, which were hooked to telephone poles, smoked briefly before being hosed down.

Though Pattybell did not cry, Olivia did. Then she stopped. To keep crying would be no more useful than to pace up and down as Curtis did, testing from time to time the closest iron pickets to see how warm they were.

She gathered Pattybell into her arms, cupped her head in one spread hand, and slowly turned her face away from the burning house and pressed it into her shoulder. How small she was!

From the fence, Curtis watched Olivia begin to rock back and forth, crooning something low and monotonous against the absurdly bright scarf.

He rested himself against the heated iron pickets and, coughing, checked that his watch had reached midnight. From this angle, he could see how his wife had enclosed the other body warmly with her own. In the uneven flickers of light, her face, he saw, was calm, even serene.

Good Will Toward Men

by Clyde Edgerton

The puppies go like hotcakes. At three hundred dollars a throw.

One of Melvin's businesses is to sell around seven thousand dollars worth of puppies a year in the month or so before Christmas. Black, yellow, chocolate labs. Four litters from his eight breeder dogs.

Melvin sits about halfway back in Duke Chapel, one hour into the *Messiah,* this song that runs three hours long and has a big choir and orchestra to do it. Melvin's hands rest in his lap, his thumbs together. The seating is tight. He wears his tweed sport coat and yellow tie. To his immediate right sits his new daughter-in-law, Kathy. She's why he's here. She insisted. Melvin thinks she's pushy; she has ideas she talks about all the time, and besides that she has big hands, these big, clean, bony hands. She's taller than his son. She's not fat, just big-boned, tall. And those big hands. Melvin doesn't know what his son sees in her. He sort of talked to his son about that, talked around it, he guesses, but there's only so much you can do once they get out on their own.

Melvin volunteers to hold many of the puppies he sells in November and December until Christmas Eve. Right now he's got only two puppies unsold, two beautiful yellow labs, and there's a week to go until Christmas Day. Yesterday he had three unsold, all females. One was a chocolate. He knew the yellows would go fastest, so when the fellow who'd come in from Raleigh dressed in a shirt and tie said he didn't know which one to pick, Melvin suggested the chocolate—whose mother was Melvin's only chocolate breeder, and high-strung. Too high-strung. For every reason the yellows were the best choice, but this fellow would not do his research. Many people didn't—more than you might think. This fellow didn't even seem to know or care that the puppy's sires were on the premises—and that he could check them out. Melvin had taken his money and filled out the paperwork. The man would pick up the dog on Christmas Eve.

Just about every man in the chapel has on a coat and tie. The program shows that there is a part 1, part 2, and part 3. The choir sings each sentence written there in the program, sings it over and over and over, every which way: "Glory to God in the highest, Glory to God in the highest, and peace on earth, good will toward men. Glory to God in the highest, and peace on earth, peace on earth, peace on earth, good will toward men, good will toward men."

Now it is "His yoke is easy, and his burden is light."

The seats are hard. The intermission is next. He'll just have to . . . he'll just, by golly, have to go out and sit in his truck for the last two hours. He can idle the truck engine, stay warm. Big-pawed Kathy will just have to swallow it. He has to draw the line somewhere, and this is as good a place as any. His son didn't draw the line and is now stuck with a woman bigger than he is. Probably weighs more. She probably weighs no telling what. But no fat. She jogs. His son married a jogger. They are still singing that one line, "His yoke is easy, and his burden is light." That's about Jesus. This song was written in England a long time ago, he just read in the program, for a king—all about Jesus being on the way, then arriving. "His yoke is easy, and his burden is light." That means that even if Melvin *had* unfairly sold a few dogs, Jesus wouldn't hold it against him as long as the other fellow hadn't done his research. Jesus and his disciples were all fishermen. They wouldn't have been tenderhearted about selling a dog. They were out in the real world, too.

It was cold outside, supposed to get down to nineteen. But stuffy inside. He loosened his tie. She probably wouldn't like that, but he couldn't do everything to make her happy. The road to hell.

He remembers he has a fresh plug of Brown & Williamson in his glove compartment. That's another thing: Kathy-with-the-Big-Hands will tell him he has tobacco juice on his chin—and then reach up and wipe it off. She has a lot of nerve. Touching his face.

WHEN KATHY LEAVES to go to the bathroom at intermission, he stands and walks out. In the truck he places the rolled up program on the dash, inserts the key into the ignition, starts the truck, opens the glove compartment, gets out his plug of Brown & Williamson. He digs down into his pocket for his three-blade Case, then cuts him a good-sized plug.

The knock on the passenger window surprises him. As his eyes move to see who it is, his mind is saying, "Kathy. That Kathy." It figures. He should have just told her. But it isn't Kathy. It's, by golly, who is it? That man he sold the dog to, the chocolate! Melvin lowers the window.

"Mr. Reed," says the man, "I'm Barry Tally. I bought a dog from you yesterday—and left him for Christmas Eve pick up. Mind if I get in for just a second? It's cold out here. I was inside, too, saw you come out. I couldn't take any more."

"Well, it's cold in here, too, Mr. Tally, and I'm heading back inside. I just came out here to get something out of my glove compartment."

Kathy walks up. "I was worried about you," she says to Melvin through the open window. "Intermission is going to be over if we don't hurry back."

"I'm Barry Tally," says the man. "I just bought a dog from Mr. Reed here. A chocolate lab."

"I'm Kathy. I just married his son. You bought the last chocolate?"

"Yes, I did."

"And there were a few yellow labs left?"

"A couple—yes."

"Well," she says. She looks in at Melvin, then at Barry Tally. "Did you know the mother of your dog is very high-strung?"

"Well, no. No, I didn't. Mr. Reed here told me the chocolate was the pick of the litter." Mr. Tally rubs his hands together, blows into one balled fist, then the other, looks in at Melvin.

Melvin says to Mr. Tally, "There's a lot she don't know about dogs. You got yourself a fine dog."

"I know enough," says Kathy, "to know the yellow labs will make better pets than that chocolate."

"He wouldn't mislead me, would he?" says Barry Tally, with a short chuckle. Then he looks in at Melvin again.

"No," says Melvin. "No, sir." In his chest, he is raging.

"I wouldn't have thought so," says Kathy. She looks at her watch. "It's too late to go back in. Let's go over to the student union for coffee."

"I'm going to stay here in the truck," says Melvin.

"Then I'll be back," says Kathy. "There's room enough in the truck for three. I'll get us all coffee and be right back. How do you like your coffee, Mr. Tally? I know how he likes his."

"Just cream."

"Listen," says Melvin. "I don't want to talk to you — to either one of you. I'm too old for all of this, for all of this music and all of this talk. I'm not feeling well. I'll be here in the truck. You better go on back inside and finish the music, Kathy. Sorry, Mr. . . ."

"Tally."

"Mr. Tally. I'll be fine out here by myself. I want to be by myself. That's why I came out here. That's how it needs to be, now."

"Can we just talk through this?" Kathy asks.

"No. Go back inside. I mean it. I need to be alone now. I mean it."

MELVIN CLOSES THE window. What were those words? he thinks. His yoke is light? He wouldn't get bothered about something like selling a dog. And He wouldn't allow a big-boned woman to work on His head, either.

He picks up the program from the dashboard. He reads, "Peace on earth, good will toward men." He rolls down his window, spits, rolls the window back up, looks at a streetlight down there ahead, a light through some bare black limbs. Good will. Good will toward men. Maybe there are some things, somewhere, where you need to explain what the other guy doesn't know.

Christmas on Madewell Mountain

by Donald Harington

There was already snow on the ground.

Why hadn't Sugrue thought to buy her some mittens or gloves? He had filled that storeroom—Adam's bedroom—with enough food and supplies and presents for her to last for a long, long time: he must have been planning to keep her for years. But he had neglected to get so many things that she would need, and hadn't even thought of Kool-Aid and scissors and paper and books, and he hadn't seemed to realize that she would outgrow all the clothes he'd bought for her.

Thinking of Christmas coming, Robin decided to go ahead and open everything he'd bought, searching for gloves or mittens, and while this would spoil the surprise of opening things he'd intended to give her for Christmas or Valentine's or Easter or her next birthday or whenever, the whole idea of surprise and whatever fun is in the surprise means that there has to be another person involved, and there wasn't any other person anymore. Even with Hreapha and Robert in the bed with her each night, she had moments of panic at the thought that she was all alone now. Anyhow, being all alone allowed her to go ahead and open all the boxes and all the bags and see all the stuff that Sugrue had intended to give her for presents eventually. "Thank you, thank you," she kept saying to him again and again, as she opened the packages, which even included a box of ribbon candy intended for Christmas. Having learned no longer to believe in the Tooth Fairy, she was now prepared to accept this answer to her burning question, How could Santa Claus possibly find her this far off in the wilderness? She saw plenty of evidence that Sugrue had intended to be Santa, just as he had once been the Tooth Fairy. He had really got her some nice things, and she was sorry that he'd never be around to see her play with them or put them on . . . unless his ghost was here, and she surely had no awareness of his ghost being around, except for that ghastly skeleton in the outhouse, all that remained of him after the buzzards, crows, and vermin had eaten him.

Why didn't she just get rid of the skeleton, which wasn't too heavy for her to drag off its perch? It certainly wasn't because she was afraid to touch it, because after all she'd made sure that those finger bones had wrapped around the neck of that whiskey bottle. And the skeleton as such didn't scare her. She remembered Halloweens when some of the kids dressed themselves in skeleton costumes, which she had thought were the least frightful of all possible costumes. What is scary about a collection of bones? No, maybe there were only two reasons she had decided to leave the skeleton there: one was that the outhouse had been Sugrue's favorite place, where he had spent an awful lot of time. Dozens of times when she'd needed to go, she had opened the outhouse door to find him sitting there reading an old issue of *Police Gazette* and she could only say "oops" and shut the door and wait for him to come out. But the other reason, the main reason, was that she liked the idea of leaving the skeleton there as a reminder that this man, Sugrue Alan, who had brought this world into existence, had kidnapped her away from her mother and friends and taken her to live in this place, was now no longer alive. She wanted to be able at any time to glance in the direction of the outhouse and see that reminder sitting there with that stupid grin and that stupid bottle of stupid whiskey in his hand.

Whenever Adam wasn't around—that is, whenever she couldn't detect that he was present, which quite often he was not, she just had to talk to Hreapha or Robert, or to herself. "I need to grow up fast," she said one day, to any ears that cared to hear it. Her own ears did: she was painfully aware of how little and helpless and innocent she was, and she wanted to become an adult as soon as she could. But the more she thought about it, and wondered how long it would take for her to become an adult, the more she understood that what she really, really wanted, more than anything else in the world, was just to stay the age she was right now forevermore. Just not ever change, just always be little and fragile and simple.

She knew she spent too much time thinking. And too much thinking wasn't good for her. She tried to avoid it by spending as much time as she could with her two precious books, the old *Cyclopaedia*, filled with all kinds of handy hints on how to live and manage a homestead, and the Bible, filled with all kinds of interesting stories.

Much of the *Cyclopaedia* was either over her head ("Farm Fences," "Making Our Own Fertilizers," "Caponizing") or useless ("The Best Known Recipe for Corning Beef," "To Banish Crows from a Field," "How to Judge a Horse"), but there were pages and pages of things she ought to know ("How to Keep Sweet Potatoes," "Winter Egg Production," "To Stop Bleeding," "Washing Made Easy," "Burns and Scalds"), and there were hundreds of recipes to be tried out, and she proceeded each day to try a new one: hominy fritters and potato cakes for breakfast, chicken patties and potato salad for lunch. There was something called "Sauce Robert," easy, with onions from the supply she'd helped Sugrue harvest and dry last summer, a recipe that she couldn't resist making and trying out on her kitty, who liked it if it was poured over protein like chicken or ham. There were desserts galore she tried. There were sixty different recipes for pudding, but she had the ingredients for less than half of them, which was more than she could eat. Her favorite was called "Kiss Pudding," using mostly egg yolks (which was spelled "yelks" throughout the book). There was a simple recipe "To Cook a Rabbit," so with Hreapha's help she went out and shot a rabbit and cooked it according to the directions and it was delicious, although not that much different from chicken. One dish that was different somewhat from chicken was the pigeon pie. She used the

.22 rifle to kill a few pigeons. The recipe called for lining the bottom of the dish with a veal cutlet or rump steak, which she did not have, so she substituted ham, and it was just fine. She always shared her dishes with Hreapha and Robert, who greatly appreciated them.

She also took her mind off of thinking too much by playing with her paper dolls in her paper town of Stay More. The problem was that her paper dolls talked to her, just as Adam did. Oh, of course it was probably just her own voice, but the paper dolls, those old country people of Stay More named Ingledew and Swain and Whitter and Duckworth and Coe and Dinsmore and Chism and so on, people Sugrue had endlessly told her about, seemed to be talking to her in voices that weren't her own, that she couldn't even imitate, because they were country voices, like Adam's. They told her stories that she couldn't possibly have made up by herself, stories about floods and droughts and periods of darkness and periods of light, and an unforgettable picnic and the organization of a Masonic lodge—surely she couldn't have been making all of this up in play-like. But she distinctly heard their voices. "Hreapha, can't you hear them too?" she asked, but her adorable dog just cocked her head to one side as if she were trying to listen, without acknowledging the voices.

For the longest time she had persuaded herself that the voice of the ghost Adam Madewell was just something she was imagining, although she couldn't imagine how she would have been able to know the particular way he talked and some of the words he used.

But how could she explain his finding those two books for her? Did she just have a hunch to see what was beyond that little door in the ceiling of the kitchen and go up there with her flashlight and find those two books? Well, it wasn't impossible, but she was pretty well convinced that there really was a ghost named Adam who sometimes talked to her. And what about that business of singing the "Farther Along" hymn? She had heard Sugrue make some references to it, but he'd never sung it, so how did she learn the words and tune, unless she learned them from Adam?

She loved that song, and every day she sang it; she even sang it in bed at night when she was trying to go to sleep. She understood that "Farther Along" was a funeral hymn and ought to be reserved for funerals, but day by day the people in her paper town of Stay More began to die, of natural causes or illnesses or whatever people died of, including murder, and while she didn't actually try to bury the paper dolls, she had a little memorial service for those who died and she sang "Farther Along."

And when she got to that lovely verse that said "When we see Jesus coming in glory, When He comes from His home in the sky; Then we will meet Him in that bright mansion, We'll understand it all by and by," she always began to wonder if this old house in which she lived might possibly be That Bright Mansion. She had never seen a mansion; her hometown had some fancy houses but not any mansions, which she knew were supposed to be very large and very imposing, neither of which this old house was. Still, she began to think that perhaps when Jesus came to meet her in this house, the house would be transformed into a mansion, just as pumpkins could be transformed into coaches in "Cinderella."

Robin was ready for Jesus. She took the Bible and, avoiding all those stories about unpronounceable names like Zelophehad, Ahinoam, Zedekiah, and Athaliah, began at the beginning of the New Testament and read the four gospels. It took her a week to read each one, but by then according to the Ouija board it was Christmas, appropriately, because she could celebrate the first Christmas in her life in which the meaning of the day had real significance as the birthday of the nice interesting kind man named Jesus, who was called the Christ.

She had got out the Ouija board again and with Hreapha's help determined that Christmas of this year was only three days away. She took the axe and cut down a little cedar tree behind the house and figured out a way to make it stand up in the living room, "planting" it in one of the wooden bails from the cooper's shed. "Adam, do you mind if I borrow this?" she asked, but got no answer. She decorated her Christmas tree with stars that she made out of toilet paper tubes (although she never used the outhouse anymore, she still used toilet paper) and colored with her crayons, which were in danger of being used up. Searching through the storeroom for the possibility that Sugrue might have bought more than one big box of crayons, she came upon a paper sack she'd overlooked before. In it were a half dozen ears of dried-up yellow corn, and there was a note, hand-lettered on a piece of brown paper, which said, "These here is popcorn, for you to eat or maybe make you some strings for your Christmas tree. Sorry there's no oranges to put in your stocking but I got you some ribbon candy somewhere around in here. Merry Christmas and love, Sugrue." Before she shelled the kernels from the ears and attempted to pop them, she had to spend just a little time crying. Then when her tears were dry, she put some of the popcorn in a pot and popped it, and spent the rest of the day stringing it on coarse cotton thread (although Sugrue had never thought to have bought some scissors, he'd stocked a supply of other sewing things, like needles and thread). Thus her Christmas tree was garlanded with white fluffy strings of popcorn. It was the prettiest Christmas tree she'd ever had. She had a bit of trouble keeping Robert from climbing the tree, but she scolded him about it, and he left it alone, although when he thought she wasn't looking he took a swat or two at one of the dangling stars.

The next day she took the shotgun and the turkey caller and went off with Hreapha (she had to shut Robert in the house to keep him from going too, commanding him to stay off the Christmas tree) to find a wild turkey for Christmas dinner, although she'd eaten so many leftovers from Thanksgiving that she was really tired of turkey and didn't care whether she found one or not. The *Cyclopaedia* had a great recipe for roast partridge and another recipe for a bread sauce for partridges, but she had no idea what a partridge was, apart from the "Twelve Days of Christmas" song. There was a pear tree up in the old orchard (which hadn't borne any fruit this year), and she looked there first for the partridge. "Hreapha, do you know what a partridge looks like?" she asked. Poor Hreapha looked very sorrowful not to be able to help, but Robin assumed that one bird was the same as the next to her.

The snow in the woods was deep in places, and they couldn't go very far. Robin didn't even bother with the turkey caller. She decided just to serve ham for Christmas and turned around and headed back toward the house. Suddenly a large bird of some kind flew up out of the leaves and landed on the limb of an oak, and she loaded the shotgun with one shell and aimed it and fired, and the bird was hit. She didn't know if it was a partridge or maybe a prairie chicken or grouse or quail or what.

But she plucked all the feathers off and washed it and stuffed it and prepared to cook it according to the *Cyclopaedia*'s recipe for partridge. Christmas morning they woke early because of the brightness: it had snowed during the night and the sunlight was reflecting off the snow and brightening up everything ("In that bright mansion," she sang). Still entertaining a shred of hope that Santa might somehow have found her house, she ran to the Christmas tree, but could only stand there pretending, "Oh look!

A bicycle!" She realized there really wasn't any place she could ride a bicycle in this weedy wilderness. "Oh look! Skis!" she exclaimed and sat down to try them on. Hreapha and Robert observed her oddly. "Merry Christmas, Hreapha!" she said. "Here's a sweater I knitted for you!" and she pretended to put the play-like sweater on Hreapha. She noticed that Hreapha's belly was really swollen. "Merry Christmas, Robert!" she said. "Here's a toy mouse I got for you to chase!" and she wound up the make-believe toy mouse and set it free, but Robert wouldn't chase it. She was sorry that animals couldn't make-believe. She had gift-wrapped just a few of the presents that Sugrue had intended to give her, which were real, not make-believe, and she slowly opened them and thanked him for each one.

She could not help wondering what she might actually have received at Christmas from her mother (and maybe even her father too, if he came, or sent something). She wondered how much her mother missed her, and thought that possibly her mother had even gone ahead and wrapped gifts for her even though she wasn't there. But she was proud of herself for putting together such a good Christmas without any help from her mother.

She'd left three of Sugrue's long socks (which she'd laundered) tacked to the wall beside the stove and filled them with ribbon candy and popcorn balls made with sugar syrup. Hreapha's stocking also had in it some of the Purina dog chow (which was running low), and Robert's stocking had a can of tuna fish, and the animals were really able to appreciate the edible contents of their stockings, except the ribbon candy, which they wouldn't eat.

Robin put the partridge (if that's what it was) in the oven to bake. The sun was so bright they went out to play in the snow for a while, and Robin decided to see if they could go as far as the beaver pond, to wish a merry Christmas to their beaver friends. She had to carry Robert because the snow was too deep for him, but it wasn't too deep for Hreapha, who managed to sort of leap in and out of it. They reached the pond to find it covered with ice, but there was an opening through the ice near the beaver's lodge, and when Robin called "Merry Christmas!" a few times the family of beaver came up through that hole in the ice and even attempted to walk on the ice, which was too slippery for them. But Hreapha barked her "Hreapha!" and Robert mewed his "Woo! Woo!" and they were all one big happy family for a little while until Robin began to get very cold, and they just barely made it back to the house before freezing to death.

She had to warm up and dry off at the stove for a long time before she could resume preparing the Christmas dinner. When it was ready, just as she had done at Thanksgiving, she sat Hreapha and Robert at the table and tied little napkins around their necks. She said a kind of grace, "Dear Jesus, I have got to know you pretty good by reading about you, and I do believe you're here with us on your birthday, aren't you? Thank you for being here, Jesus, and thank you for all this food and for keeping us warm and safe. If there was anything I could ask for, it would be that you would let Adam be here too. Happy birthday, Jesus, and merry Christmas. Amen."

She waited just a few moments, and then called, "Adam? Adam! Don't you want to eat Christmas dinner with us?" There was no answer. She said, "Well, I'm being silly, because ghosts don't eat anything. Do they?"

And his voice replied! *I ain't no ghost, you dizzy gal. Ghosts is dead people, I ain't never been dead, though I've felt close to it sometimes.*

"Merry Christmas, Adam!" she said.

Merry Christmas to you, Miss Robin. You've sure been doing it up proud the way my maw would've done, with them popcorn balls and all.

"I'm sorry you can't eat with us, but I'll set a plate out for you anyhow."

Thank ye kindly. Howsomever, that ain't no partridge. It's jist a big fat bobwhite. I'll bet it tastes real good anyhow.

They had a nice fine dinner and everybody was happy and after dinner there was just one more thing Robin wanted to do for Christmas. She took a shovel and found the spot under the porch where Sugrue had said he'd buried the money box. She started digging it up. Hreapha stepped in and helped and was a faster digger than Robin, although her swollen belly hampered her and tired her out. They dug up the box and took it into the house, and Robin used the key that Sugrue had given her.

Just for the fun of it, and with nothing better to do for a couple of hours, she counted all the money, which was mostly in hundred dollar bills, four thousand and twenty of them. She might not ever be able to spend any of it. But it sure was nice to have that much, nearly half a million.

"Thank you, Sugrue," she said. "Merry Christmas."

The Perfect Tree

by Carolyn Haines

Death and anger lay between them deeper than the Mississippi River she crossed in the hazy light of a warm December dawn. He was her brother, and once again he'd figured a way to ruin Christmas.

Alice, her best friend in Boulder, had handed her a Thermos of coffee and a bit of advice. "There's always one member in each family who steals Christmas," she'd said. "Just remember, he can't take more than you're willing to give him. You do what you've got to do and hurry back out here. Don't linger, Rita. That kudzu will crawl right over you, tangle you up, and trap you if you let it. Just do what you feel you must and get the hell out of there."

What did she owe Richard? That was the question Rita pondered as she drove across the river and into Mississippi. What was the total of the debt she'd incurred for leaving Wiggins and having a halfway decent life? Richard's tabulations would be high, and payment had come due. After fifteen years of voluntary exile, she'd been called home.

The fog lifted as she cut through the heart of the Delta. The fields were barren, waiting for the cotton that would be planted in the spring. It was an abnormally mild winter, the day temperate enough to grow a crop. But winter weather was unpredictable. The high of seventy today could be a low of twenty by night. Only kudzu and honeysuckle thrived on such harsh surprises.

In the bright sunlight that finally cut through the fog, the vista of the Delta was uninterrupted. The homes of the wealthy were set far back from the road, hidden by trees. Only shacks and shanties, many of them now abandoned, could be clearly seen in the vast expanse of the open fields. The river was on her right. At times she could see the high levee that had been built after the flood of 1927. Man had contained the river. For the moment. The Mississippi was a trickster; it could plod along for decades, docile and restrained, but it would not always be so obedient. The thought made her smile.

She stopped at noon in Yazoo City, set on a steep hill that let everyone know the flat stretches of the Delta were over. Another four hours and she'd be there, no trace of the Colorado winter left on her vehicle or her body. She'd traded her coat and gloves for a short-sleeve blouse and an open truck window.

She bought a burger at a drive-through and kept going, her foot heavier on the accelerator than before. Homing instinct, she thought with a grimace. And some people wanted to deny that humans were animals.

On Highway 49, she was surprised by the feeling of warmth that touched her at the sight of the fruit stands selling fresh produce, chowchow, fig preserves, pickled watermelon rind, orange-blossom honey, Christmas trees. There was nothing worse than a store-bought tree. Her entire childhood Christmas had been built around finding the perfect tree—the thirteen-foot cedar that almost touched the ceiling in the living room.

It had taken the whole family to put up the tree, to make it steady in the stand and then to run the strings of multicolored lights around it. Eighteen strings of lights, always tangled in the box from the year before. But no one had argued or complained.

She'd loved hanging the ornaments, the delicate glass baubles. She wondered if Richard had kept the family decorations. She'd left them, unwilling to pack any more than she already had. There had been over a hundred of the glass decorations, some dating back to her grandmother's trees. It was unlikely they'd survived Richard's alcoholic rages, and she prepared herself with no expectations. It was ridiculous to think of Christmas ornaments anyway. She hadn't come to celebrate a holiday; she was on her way home for a death watch. Richard had, at last, figured out how to force her home and steal a final Christmas.

The war he'd waged against her had been nothing compared to the campaign he'd conducted against himself. Emphysema, cirrhosis, heart damage—he'd captured them all. There was little left of the stocky athlete who'd been a champion swimmer and baseball player.

In Hattiesburg, she thought of high school, when her older

brother had been Most Popular and the guy with the quick smile and quicker temper. The country girls had found him irresistible. When had he crossed the line from popular to pathetic?

Another hour and she'd be there. Wiggins. Pickle capital of the world; one county north of the wide-open cities of the Gulf Coast. Wiggins was pines and hardwoods, thousands of wooded acres where she and Richard and their mother had searched out, every year, the perfect cedar to saw down and bring home for Christmas.

It was early afternoon when she turned off Highway 49 and took Double Branch Road into town. She forced herself to drive by their old house on the hill. Paint was scaling off it like a terminal condition. The swing was hanging by one chain. There was a blue Toyota under the portico on the side of the house, and tree limbs from the big oaks were scattered all over the yard. What would her parents say of such neglect? Somehow, they would hold her accountable.

Richard was living with a woman named Lucille. It had been Lucille who called her in Boulder, telling her that Richard was terminal and that he was asking for her. Lucille's voice was tired, worn smooth like a rock beneath fast water.

Rita drove straight to the hospital, to the surgical ward, as Lucille had directed her. There would be no surgery—there would be nothing left of Richard if they began excising the things that had gone bad. But it was the best place for him, the doctor had told her. Close to the nurses' station.

The hospital had expanded, but she found her way with only a few wrong turns. Standing outside, she listened to harsh, dragging breath coming from the room. No wonder he was tired. It was a struggle for him just to draw in air. Tapping lightly, she walked into the room. The man in bed was a stranger. Gray hair bristled on his face. The only recognizable piece of him was a calf that had slipped from beneath the covers. In the lean muscle was the athlete that had once been her powerful brother.

"Rita," he panted, his eyes almost open. "You came."

She had. Against her survival instinct and the advice of her best friend. But in Richard's eyes, it was another test passed—family before self-preservation.

"Lucille said you wanted to talk to me," she said.

"I'm going home for Christmas," he said, struggling for breath to make the words. "I wanted you home, too."

Of the many things she'd expected him to say, that wasn't it. "Well, I'm here," she fumbled. "It's hot as hell outside. Seventy, at least. In Boulder we had snow." In less than a minute, she'd fallen back on the weather. She had nothing to say to her brother. Too many things had been said in the past. Too many misunderstandings had turned into harsh judgments and unforgivable acts of cruelty and revenge. Yet she had to talk to cover his painful breathing. "Do they still decorate the cemetery with Christmas trees and garland?" Had she thought it through, she'd never have mentioned the cemetery.

"Yes," he said. "Poinsettias everywhere. Lights on the tombstones. Same as always." He breathed. "Make Lucille cremate me. Black Creek."

She knew that's where he wanted his ashes scattered. The river ran through a national forest, and there was a place of solitary wilderness where Richard had loved to camp. "Okay," she said.

"She won't want to do it. Don't let her bury me."

Was this her last task for her brother? "I promise."

"Going home tomorrow."

Was he telling her he was dying? If so, surely he was in no condition to leave the hospital? He was hooked to a bank of monitors, drips, and tubes that ran over, under, and around the bed.

"I want a tree," he said, his pale eyes focusing on her. "Thirteen feet. Not store bought." The faintest smile touched his face. "For Mama."

She understood then. He'd called her home to do the thing no one else would do.

"Where is it?" she asked, knowing that this wasn't just any tree Richard wanted. He'd spotted it, months before, like they'd done when their mother was alive. They'd ridden the back roads and the main streets, searching out the perfect tree, the one shapely on all sides. And in the dead of night, they'd gotten it, no matter where it had been growing.

"Buster McCabe," Richard said, watching her face for telltale signs of fear or weakness. He knew her so well.

"Are you really going home?" she asked to cover her sudden dizziness.

"Tomorrow. Ask the nurses."

"I need to clean up. I've been driving a long time." She walked out of the room and went to the nurses' desk.

"The doctor's releasing him to hospice care." The nurse wouldn't meet her gaze. "Mr. Jones said you had a truck and that you could get him home. They're going to send a hospital bed and some other equipment."

She left the hospital and drove toward the main street of town. At the first light she took a right on Bentley Drive and headed up a hill toward the most prestigious residential section of Wiggins. She saw the tree before she saw the McCabe house. It stood alone on a corner of the lawn, a beautiful cedar, the perfect size and shape. Richard had always had an eye for a good tree. And he'd never backed down from a challenge. That was where they'd differed the most.

She drove to the Western Motel and checked in, drawing the heavy draperies tight. She picked up the phone and called Alice.

"I made it," she said.

"What does he want?" Alice asked.

Alice knew the loops and snares of family. She, too, had run away and found a haven in the high Colorado altitude.

"He's going home to die, and he wants a Christmas tree and for me to make sure he's cremated instead of buried."

Alice considered the requests. "I guess that's not so bad. I was expecting something really crazy. I mean this is the guy who used to hold you against a wall and pretend that he was going to punch your face in."

"I was a Goody Two-shoes."

Alice snorted. "Right. So you deserved to be terrorized every time your parents' backs were turned. You'll be coming back to Boulder with more bags than you left with, I can see."

"He wants me to steal the Christmas tree from the McCabes' front lawn."

"I knew the bastard would do one last thing to hurt you." Alice's voice was tight with anger. "Hell, he's dying. Buy a damn tree. He'll never know."

Rita rolled the phone cord around her finger. "It's a perfect tree."

"You're thinking of doing it." Alice was shocked. "Times aren't like they were when your folks were alive. People go to jail for trespassing and property damage."

"I can get it."

"That bastard has issued one final challenge and you're going to be suckered into taking it."

"One year, we found the perfect tree in a car lot on Main Street, but we knew we couldn't get it in a pickup truck because of the streetlights. Mama borrowed the old hearse from the funeral home. We cruised down Main Street and jumped out of the back of the hearse like a swat team. It was the most exciting thing I've ever done. It was excellent."

"Your mother was one warped individual. No wonder you're such a mess."

"It was such fun," Rita said. "The tree was the only good thing about Christmas."

"If you get put in jail, call me." Alice was worn out with arguing. "I know you're going to do this."

"There's one other thing you should know. Buster McCabe attacked me when I was in the eighth grade. I think he was trying to rape me, but back then I just thought he was trying to beat me up. Richard beat him nearly to death. After that, Buster told people that Richard stole things from his father's store. Richard didn't steal. Everyone in town began to believe he did, though."

There was a silence. "Jesus. Could things be more fucked up between you and your brother? Look, just do whatever it is you have to do and get out of that town."

"I'll be home soon." Rita hung up, undressed, and got under the covers. In the darkness she slept and dreamt, transported back to childhood and fleeting moments of colored lights and tinsel, of anticipation and fear.

SHE MET THE doctor in the corridor outside her brother's room when he made evening rounds. He was young and sincere. Richard's body was giving up in increments. He wanted to go home to smoke and drink. Why not?

She was still standing there when she saw Charlie approaching. Charlie, the good cousin, the scholarship winner, the bright one, the one who never participated in the Christmas tree thefts or the practical jokes of water balloons and burning paper sacks of dog excrement.

"Has he asked you?" Charlie's face was furrowed with worry. "It's ludicrous. We can't steal a tree from someone's front lawn."

She was surprised yet again. So Richard had drawn the noose of an illegal act around Charlie also. Whatever his physical condition, Richard was having a blast emotionally. It had taken dying, but he'd finally snared the two of them, she thought.

"How can we not do it? It's his last request."

"If he asked you to kill someone, would you?" Charlie was logical.

"Stealing a Christmas tree hardly compares to murder."

"I remember the year you and Aunt Greta and Richard stole that cedar tree out of the cemetery. And the year you snatched the one out of Renfroe's car lot on Main Street in the old hearse. I'm not getting involved with you Joneses. Y'all have never been right. I loved Aunt Greta, but she had no respect for the law or decent behavior."

"I didn't ask Richard to want that tree," Rita said, "but it's more than the tree. There's a score to settle here."

"With a cedar tree?" Charlie asked in frustration. "What did the tree ever do to you?"

"With Buster McCabe."

"He's the mayor now."

"Even better," she said.

Charlie put his hand on her shoulder. "The past is gone, Rita. If you don't let it go, you're going to end up just like Richard. It's not the whiskey or the cigarettes that's killed him, it's the past."

"I know." She reached up and put her hand over his. "But maybe part of exorcising the past is finally standing up to it."

"That's an excuse. You left here. You made something of yourself. Don't throw it all away now."

"Maybe, in his own way, Richard knows something we don't."

"Richard holds a grudge better than anyone I've ever known. I don't have to remind you that he hasn't called you in fifteen years."

She knew then that he wouldn't help with the tree. He would do the right thing by Richard, but stealing a tree wasn't part of the bargain. She was on her own.

"What's Lucille like?" she asked.

"Quiet." He gave her shoulder one last squeeze before he removed his hand. "He won't last long at home." When she didn't say anything, he started away. "Call me when they release him. The nurses said it should be around eleven."

She went into the hospital room. Richard was asleep, fighting for each breath, purplish hands and feet twitching. She tucked his hands under the blanket and left. She made one loop through the town. Nothing had really changed. It was seven o'clock in the evening and Wiggins was dead. She drove to Bentley Drive.

Parking the truck a block away from the tree, she walked slowly up the street, her eye on the cedar. It was in the corner of the McCabe front yard not far from a streetlight. The lawn was large and well manicured with azaleas around the house and a magnolia tree to the right by a sunroom that had been enclosed. The house was two stories, and the front window looked out right at the cedar tree. The lawn rolled gently to the street and a three-foot stone embankment that would work in her favor if she could manage to back the pickup truck there without being seen.

A woman, tiny and blond, opened the front door, pulling a sweater more tightly around her body as she waited for a small dog to run out and pee. Rita kept walking, making her strides long. She hadn't thought that Buster would be married. It had never occurred to her that he'd find a woman willing to bind herself legally to him.

She drove to the Wal-Mart and bought a limb saw. A chain saw would work much faster, but she couldn't afford the noise. The trunk of the tree was about five inches. She'd have to work fast and hard to get it down and away without being caught. Dragging the tree into the bed of the truck was the best possible plan. The big cedar would be too heavy for her to haul very far by herself. It was risky, but it was doable.

On the way out of Wal-Mart, she picked up a pot of poinsettias. At the cemetery, she had no trouble finding the graves where her parents lay side by side. She put the flowers between them and saw that someone had already strung a garland filled with miniature lights around their headstones. Battery operated, the tiny white lights gave a holiday twinkle. Perhaps Lucille had done it.

She went back to the motel, pulled the drapes again, and slept.

The alarm woke her at one A.M. In coming back to Wiggins, she'd lost all touch with the normal rhythms of her life. She dressed and then slipped outside into the warm, inky blackness of the night. The saw was on the truck seat beside her with her leather gloves.

Two blocks from the McCabes', she turned off the truck lights. The town was dead asleep. Moving slowly, she drove past the house, stopped, and began to back up to the embankment. Headlights turned onto the street three blocks down. A vehicle was slowly cruising toward her.

Heart pounding, she turned on her lights and drove away. It took another twenty minutes of driving through town to convince herself it was okay to go back. As she turned onto Bentley Drive, she killed her lights once again. The house was dark, shuttered looking, as she drove by, stopped, and prepared to back up.

The knock at the passenger window almost made her scream.

It took her a moment to recognize Charlie. She let the window down.

"Don't stop here," he said. "Go down a block."

She didn't argue. She drove down and parked on the street, letting the tailgate down before she joined him by the embankment.

"I'll saw, you pull the tree toward you. We can both drag it to the truck."

"Okay," she said. This was the way it had been in childhood, except it had been Richard giving the orders while her mother waited in the get-away vehicle. She swallowed the rush of excitement and put on her gloves. Without another word she waded into the sticky fronds of the cedar and began working her hands around the trunk. Charlie was at the base, already sawing.

The night was so still, the sound of the saw seemed to echo down the street. She kept her gaze on the front door of the house, expecting at any moment that it would fly open and light would pour out on them. She felt the tree give a little, and she worked her way farther up the trunk, putting her weight into it. Charlie was sawing madly and grunting with exertion. She giggled. It was insane. What they were doing was totally insane. Charlie laughed, too, trying to stifle it so he could work.

The tough cedar snapped and the tree sagged. She levered it toward the ground as Charlie freed the final strands that held the tree to its stump.

"Let's go," he said.

They grabbed lower limbs and headed for the street, the tree a black shadow that nipped at them, following reluctantly behind. Rita pulled with all her strength, wondering what she would have done if Charlie hadn't shown up, wondering why he had.

They loaded the tree and climbed into the truck, Rita behind the wheel. Two blocks down the street, they exploded with laughter. Charlie offered her his flask of bourbon, and they drove to the old house where Rita had spent her childhood.

"What now?" she asked. The house was dark. Lucille, the woman she'd never met, was sound asleep.

"Leave it behind the tool shed for tonight. We'll get it in to-morrow and have it decorated before Richard comes home."

"Thanks, Charlie."

"Merry Christmas, Rita. It's good to see you home again."

"I won't stay."

"You shouldn't."

She got out of the truck and together they pulled the tree out. Charlie held it up while she stepped back.

"It's the perfect tree," she said.

The Gift of Lies

by Nanci Kincaid

My mother left when I was eleven. Marty and Click were still kids. She was mainly leaving Daddy, I think. But that meant she was leaving us too. Her three oldest. At first we spent a lot of time wishing she would come back. We spent a lot of time regretting whatever it was that made her leave. If she did come back we swore we'd do better by her next time. Click would stop wetting the bed every night. Marty would quit smart talking. I would develop better personal habits and appreciate things. We'd be older. Smarter.

I don't think it was because of Daddy's lies. Daddy didn't actually start lying until after Mother was gone. But she would never have understood about his lies. She was not in any mood to understand. She only understood certain things. I'm not exactly sure what. Things she thought Daddy—and the rest of us—didn't understand. Maybe that's why she finally gave up and left, took Juan with her. Juan wasn't even a year old. He had eight teeth and was just starting to hold on to things and pull himself up. He was pie-faced and as blond as me. We hardly got a chance to know him before they were gone.

Daddy keeps Juan's baby pictures in his dresser drawer. We can look at them whenever we want to. He looks like a baby who should be named Billy or Ed. Not Juan. We don't have one drop of Spanish blood in us either—none of us. So why Mother insisted on naming our baby brother Juan, nobody knows. In a way, she was telling a lie herself.

Mother left with Mike Ward. He was our neighbor. His wife, Linda, went to church where we used to go. She has three kids. They hate us now like we're the ones who ran off with their daddy. For the longest time afterward, Linda Ward would come over here to see Daddy after she got her kids put to bed at night. She wanted him to explain things.

Marty and Click and I sat on the bunk beds in their dark bedroom and listened to Mrs. Ward beg Daddy for answers. She cried and her voice shook. She spilled the cup of coffee he tried to give her. We heard it hit the floor. We heard Daddy go in the kitchen for napkins to mop up the spill. "What am I supposed to do?" she kept shouting, as if Daddy knew the answer to that.

She wanted Daddy to call Mother up and tell her to come back home and bring Mike with her. But Daddy had no idea where Mother had gone. Mrs. Ward wanted him to get in his car and go after them, bring them both back and shame them or shoot them, either one. She had all kinds of ideas. She was like a melting candle, Mrs. Ward, her voice hot and waxy, her words firey—then soft, losing their shape and meaning. Daddy was no help. He was useless.

When Mother left she wrote Daddy a note saying she had made a terrible mistake marrying him in the first place and deeply regretted her mistake, but had a chance to start her life over. Daddy sat and read and reread that letter every single night for a month afterward. It was like he thought she'd left him a secret message in invisible ink—and if he stared at it long enough it would say she loved him deeply and always would and regretted that life had forced them apart this way. I think it was wanting a lie from her so bad that made him start telling lies of his own.

My brother Marty said he was going to steal that letter as soon as he could, set a match to it, so that Daddy couldn't read it anymore. Marty would get mad when he saw Daddy reading that letter. He'd go crazy—bang his head on the bed or kick the wall with his cowboy boots until he busted a hole in the Sheetrock. It was horrible to see. Crying would have been easier, but Marty didn't really believe in boys crying. Instead he just tore something to pieces with his bare hands. Anything. A comic book or school book or the pillow on his bed, feathers flying everywhere.

For hours on end Daddy sat in his new reading glasses squinting at the parting words our mother left him. They seemed to shock him all over again every night. It was like he opened the envelope with no idea of what the letter might say. Then read it in total disbelief.

I was the one who took the letter out of Daddy's sock drawer and hid it under my mattress. I'm the oldest. It was my job to do something. I was scared to destroy the letter though. What if

Daddy needed that bad news to keep him alive? What if he would die without being able to read *I am leaving you* written in Mother's perfect handwriting?

Daddy was furious when he discovered the letter missing. He tried to make one of us confess to taking it, but we pleaded innocent. I lied, straight-faced. There was nothing he could do but spank us, hard. He took off his belt to hit us with, which he had never done before, and whipped us so long and with such fury that we all cried and he did too.

That night I got the letter out from it's hiding place. At the bottom of it Mother wrote, *PS. Tell the children I love them.* I read that maybe fifty times, trying to trick myself into believing it.

I WAS NINE when things first started going wrong. It was the Christmas I got the Bride Doll. It was a bad shock. I had never asked for any such thing. I'd asked for this toy microscope out of the Sears catalog where you could look at blood and spit and see stuff swimming around in it. Mrs. Ward's son, Avery, had one and had let me look into it. We were friends back then. So I was counting on the microscope, looking forward to studying slides of my own sweat and pee and the dog poop I had easy access to in our animal-infested yard. I wasn't expecting the Bride Doll. I wasn't expecting my mother to be more thrilled with my present than I was.

The Bride Doll was blond, pink-skinned, and blue-eyed — like me after a bath. She had an elaborate white dress and veil, immaculate hair that practically glowed in the dark, and a large plastic diamond on her red-tipped finger. There are Christmas pictures in the family album where I look dumbstruck holding up this doll for the camera. The doll is smiling. I'm not.

My mother delighted in this doll. I would go so far as to say she loved it even. The way she admired it and looked at it from all angles made me feel terrible about myself. I guess it made her feel terrible about herself too because she said, "I always dreamed I'd wear a dress like this on my wedding day." It was the first I knew that her wedding picture where she and Daddy are standing together in gray suits disappointed her. I swear, if you look at her face in that picture she just looks nervous—not miserable like she claimed later. "At least I'll get to see you wear a white dress like that someday, won't I, Kendall?"

"Yes ma'am," I said, although I had my doubts.

I don't know if I understood that the Bride Doll was a prophecy—that she illustrated all that I was to aspire to. I do remember not knowing how to play with her. It seemed wrong to undress her the way I did my Tiny Tears or any of my other nappy-headed, legless, chronically naked dolls. She wasn't a baby doll after all. She was a woman doll.

I perched the Bride Doll on my bed in all her wedding regalia and dared my uncivilized brothers to touch her or sneak a look under her skirt where she had on nothing but a cheap pair of cotton underpants. I did not want her defiled in any way. I wanted her to stay beautiful—which seemed her whole purpose for existing. I didn't want Marty and Click's dirty hands crumpling her crinoline, leaving smudges on her lily whiteness, knocking one of her curls loose, losing her small, perfect rubber shoes. She was a virgin doll. I understood that without understanding it at all. Her virtue was mine to preserve. That much I knew by pure instinct.

Click was sort of fascinated with the Bride Doll too, like Mother was. Right away he wanted to feed her something, to see if she would pee. I had to practically break his arm to keep him from dousing her with a cup of lime Kool-Aid. I had never had anything so nice before that he could not even touch it. It made him more interested than ever. "Can I hold her?" he asked me a thousand times.

"No," I said a thousand times. "Go play with your stuff. Go tear something up. Go break something to pieces."

The way Click looked at that Bride Doll sometimes, I mean, he was only four, but it seemed like he might be in love with that doll. Really. He just stared at her sometimes for such a long time, like he was waiting for her to speak his name, to say something thoughtful. It gave me the creeps. It was like he was mesmerized by her rubberized beauty, her untouchability. I think he was bewildered that a sister like me would have in my grimy possession a glorious doll like this. It made no sense to him. Or me.

The truth was that such beauty should not have been trusted to a girl like me—I was unworthy. I knew it better than anybody. I had dirt under my fingernails, mosquito bites on my legs that I had clawed into scabs, sun-bleached hair I only washed when my mother made me. Afterwards I tamed my hair with one of those plastic headbands where the little teeth bite into your scalp. Sometimes I forgot all about oral hygiene too. Would dampen my toothbrush to make my mother think I had brushed my teeth and see how long it would take her to catch on. I didn't change my underwear every day either—sometimes just because it was too much trouble. Maybe I didn't feel like it.

Marty and Click knew that I was in over my head with the Bride Doll. So they didn't resist when I closed her up in my pink bedroom and set out to play with their cap guns or pocketknives or the legions of little green army men who came already armed and dangerous and inclined toward destroying something. We played killing each other mostly, my brothers and me. We played dying in new and interesting ways, falling off the picnic table, rolling under the car, drowning in the plastic wading pool, burying ourselves in pine straw, hanging ourselves with a lasso. We never tired of death. It was the most exhilarating game we knew of.

At night I would move the Bride Doll off my unmade bed and stand her against the wall until morning. I didn't want to bend her legs and make her sit on the floor and get her skirt all dirty. I stared at her many a night until I fell asleep. She was so annoying in her perfection, her silence. Even Tiny Tears, a far lesser doll, would at least cry and wet her pants.

I'd like to say I recall the moment when the Bride Doll met her demise, but that would be a lie. I suspect that under cover of darkness, locked away in my bedroom, I disrobed the would-be bride, hook and eye by hook and eye, until she stood naked in her fascinating rubber shoes staring at my glassy blue eyes with hers. I remember that her veil would not come off. It was sort of nailed to her head. My gentle efforts to free her from it were not successful. It required muscle. My yanking messed up her look-but-don't-touch hair for which southern girls — my mother included — are so famous, but to which I was yet to aspire. Any girl can tell you how traumatic a moment it is when your perfect doll's perfect hair goes the way of all dolls before her. (It was worse than *a bad hair day*. It was *a bad hair life*.) There was no redeeming a head of golden nylon hair. I'd reduced a bastion of virtue and loveliness to just another redneck, white trash chick. It was the very downfall my mother, in her way, was trying to protect me from.

There was no comb or brush or human touch deft enough to salvage a head of doll's hair. Believe me, I tried. It is the same sort of trauma that the southern girl experiences who ever believes she can "fix her hair" or "have a hairdo." Humidity will not allow it. Not even if you cement it with a can of Aqua Net like my mother tried to do. It just goes against nature — plain and simple. Still, I was stung by my mother's remark, "Kendall, what did you do to your doll's hair?" as if I were the force of nature. Before I could explain the circumstances leading up to the hair accident, my mother shook her head in grave disappointment, that look that meant *you cannot take good care of anything, can you?*

I never even named my Bride Doll. She never seemed human enough for an actual name. I had defiled her with my own two hands. She would never recover from the catastrophic loss of beauty.

There was no redemption for a loss of that magnitude. Last I recall she reluctantly joined Marty, Click, and me in our gun games. We shot her off the roof of the car, helped her crawl, wounded, into the shade under the house. She, like us, died a thousand imaginary deaths, floated face down in the ditches, her once white dress a muddied—if not bloodied—mess. As it turned out she was a pretty good sport, taking whatever we dished out, never complaining. She didn't have the cry in her that you could shake into action the way Tiny Tears did. She was the stoic sort.

Several times I recall my mother lifting the Bride Doll from where she had been slung under the sofa, or left out in the rain, or lost in the backseat of the hot car—and bringing her back to my room, trying to perch her on my bed where she belonged. And how sad it seemed to me. My mother longing for this doll to transcend her destiny.

At one point Marty discovered that not only would the Bride Doll's head twist right and left, but it would also pop clean off. You could take batting practice with it if you wanted to. Or you could pop it onto some other headless doll who'd long ago met her defeat—just for the amusement of it. Over time the Bride Doll's eyes stopped opening and closing the way they should. They sort of glazed over. But she maintained the smile on her face to the very end.

Last I remember she was lying naked in the bottom of our toy box among the battered soldiers, Tinkertoys, Lincoln Logs, and torn up toy trucks with lost wheels. Even my mother finally turned away from her in her state of nakedness and abandonment. Another failed bride.

I learned a lot about beauty from that Bride Doll. That beauty is not much fun. That nobody wants to play with you if you are too beautiful. Too clean. Too perfect. That beauty and perfection are fleeting at best—they never last. It was a great relief to know this. Especially for a girl like me. My permanent teeth had come in crooked. My teacher wrote a note home saying I needed reading glasses. I had a wart on my index finger.

The Bride Doll taught me that in the end people are more interested in stripping you bare than in admiring you in your impeccable finery. You'll be rendered naked—one way or another—and life will have happened to you the same as it does everybody else. I took comfort in that.

It was about this time that Mr. Ward first hired Mother to come to his office half days and do some typing for him. Mrs. Ward had suggested it. She hates herself for that now. She knew Mother had been a secretary before she married Daddy and cluttered up her life with two rowdy sons and a daughter who didn't know how to take care of anything.

The first big fight I remember was when Daddy tried to make Mother quit her job. She had taken her half-day, half-pay job and stretched it out until most days Marty and I got home from school before she got Click picked up at kindergarten. Some days he fell asleep in the backseat of the car and other days he was grouchy and whiney because he needed a nap and never got one. Mother forgot to get milk for our cereal, or peanut butter for our sandwiches, or cupcakes for our class parties. She forgot to make sure we had fruit in our lunch bags or that we brushed our teeth or drank our orange juice. She forgot to read to us at night, to put pink sponge curlers in my hair before I went to bed, to make us say our prayers.

It was like Mother was trying to be something. A typist. That's what we thought at the time. And Daddy would not let her be that—or anything else. She started to move around Daddy like he was a roadblock in her path, like he was an obstacle to her happiness. She spent lots of afternoons whispering with Mrs. Ward about all that was wrong with Daddy. I got the feeling Mrs. Ward felt plenty sorry for Mother, married to such a man.

That spring my mother gave birth to Juan. When she named him Juan everybody was shocked. Daddy said she'd been watching too much Desi Arnaz on TV. But he didn't argue about it much. Juan's birth sort of ruined Mother's mood and disposition, not to mention her half-day, half-pay job typing for Mike Ward. She didn't make enough money to hire a baby-sitter to keep Juan while she joyfully typed three or four hours a day, which she seemed to believe was her true destiny. She got so frustrated staying at home all day that her breast milk dried up too soon and she had to put Juan on the bottle before he was ready. This upset Daddy. Some nights Juan screamed so bad when Mother tried to give him his bottle that Daddy would take him out of her arms and go sit outside on the porch and feed Juan himself. The fresh air seemed to calm Juan down. Mother moped around the house day after day, sad, making us feel like maybe Juan had ruined her life. Maybe we all had. For lunch she gave us bags of cheese curls or those little individual boxes of Frosted Flakes and Raisin Bran to eat dry. And almost every night she heated up Salisbury steak TV dinners. We never complained either. Only Daddy did. "I need some real food," he said.

"I need a real life," she answered.

It stayed like this until the following Christmas. It seemed like the thought of the holidays finally lifted Mother's spirits some. She did all the usual Christmas stuff like decorate the tree, make cookies, send cards, hang stockings, hide presents. By now Juan had gotten used to things and stopped most of his screaming. Mother was back in her regular clothes and had started putting on lipstick and brushing her hair every morning like she used to before Juan was born. We were having pimento cheese sandwiches or tuna fish and carrot sticks for lunch again. Marty, Click, and I made our Christmas wish lists the same as always. They wanted assorted weapons, more guns and swords and real knives. Firecrackers if they could get them. Anything that had potential to do serious bodily harm. Me, I asked for a ukelele. I don't know why.

On Christmas morning Mother was the first one up. "Smile," she said with camera in hand, as we raced to look under the tree. Sure enough, my brothers' lust for violence had been appeased. They got an assortment of toy weaponry including slingshots and bows and arrows with real tips, which would most likely be aimed at me—I could be blind within the week—not to mention the standard cap guns and toy rifles. Without warning, my distracted parents ignored my request for a ukelele and dared to give me a doll again. Maybe they thought I hadn't learned my lesson with the first doll. I know I thought they hadn't learned theirs. It was like the second chance I never wanted. This time I got a smaller "teen-age" type doll, sort of a precursor to Barbie, I guess. She wasn't nearly so elegant and inspiring as the Bride Doll had been. She looked like her wedding day had never crossed her mind. In fact, she was clearly destined for eternal adolescence like so many girls I knew—myself included. She was not a beautiful doll. She was simply *cute*. Cute is easier on everybody.

This new teenage doll was strangely unintimidating. She came with a change of outfits too, which allowed me to undress and re-dress her relatively guilt-free since she seemed designed for exactly that. It was about all I could ever think to do with a doll anyway. Maybe if I'd had an older sister or something I could have been trained into more sophisticated methods of doll play, but left to my own devices I was pathetically unimaginative.

"Santa just could not resist that doll," Mother smiled. "Look. She comes with her own plastic suitcase and a tiny change purse."

I nodded a sullen yes.

I was not the one who noticed that this *cute* doll was seriously flawed. Weeks went by and I was totally oblivious to any deficien-cies. It was my rich friend, Mary Pat, whose daddy was a doctor and who had her own horse and a swimming pool in her backyard, who pointed out—as only rich girls can—the inferiority of my Christmas present. It seemed my doll's arms didn't match in length. Well, it didn't *seem*. Her arms *didn't* match. One was too long and one was too short. It was awful. How had I missed such a glaring defect? Hadn't I studied her anatomy, little swells of minibreasts and all, enough to detect this tragic flaw? Obviously not. But once it was pointed out to me I became obsessed with it. I couldn't see anything but those mismatched arms, reaching for me, day and night. Couldn't sleep for thinking about them. All night I wrestled with the injustice of it. That my doll had to have mismatched arms, that *I* had to have a doll with mismatched arms. We both deserved better.

When I realized how imperfect my teenage doll was, it was clear we had been cheated, my parents and me. It was an unspoken rule that dolls should come perfect—that we had a right to expect at least that from any doll we spent good money on. Who in their right mind would buy a deformed doll? It was like a trick had been played on us. A mockery made of the concept of the Christmas gift. The whole purpose of a new doll was her initial perfection, wasn't it? It was the doll owner who should have the privilege of messing her up, right? Wasn't that what we were actually buying— the privilege?

I begged my mother to take this cute doll—who was less cute by the minute—back to the store and trade her for a finer phys- ical specimen. I tried again and again to explain to my parents (and Santa Claus by implication) that they had been swindled. And so had I.

My mother was appalled—not at the deficient doll—but at me. She refused to discuss the glaring deformity. She insisted that mismatched arms were an endearing quality in a doll, a sign that she was not ordinary and boring like the masses of perfectly proportioned dolls turned loose into this world. This doll was special. My mother tried hard to make me celebrate the glory of imperfection. "Pretty is as pretty does," she said.

I wish I could say I rose to the occasion and embraced this Barbie forerunner in all her prepubescent gangliness and misproportion. But I think it was around this time that I lost interest in dolls altogether.

In due time this guileless teenage doll too became victim of my brothers and my make-believe mayhem. We freckled her with a bevy of BBs, war-painted her face with Magic Markers. Slung her on top of the roof to keep the dog from chewing her mismatched arms off her pink torso. Is she still there, baked—perhaps melted— by the southern sun onto the shingles of our old house?

First I could not love the Bride Doll because she was too beautiful, too wonderful and glorious. She made me feel stupid and ugly. She made me feel clumsy and dirty. Even after I had initiated her into the nasty ways of this world I'm not sure I ever learned to love her. I never forgot how perfect she had once been. I never was able to forgive her for it.

And then came this cute doll. She was not stuck up. She was friendly. She had a change of clothes as a sort of invitation. She didn't make you feel guilty about anything. She was not a baby doll or a woman doll—she was caught in between, like so many of us have been for longer than we like to admit. But she had those arms—one too long, one too short. And that did it. I could not love her because she embarrassed me with her gross imperfection. I felt that her glaring deformity was not just hers to bear—but mine too.

It was less than a month after that Christmas that Mother left the note for Daddy saying she was going off to start a better life with Mike Ward, saying she loved Mike Ward in a way she'd never loved anybody. She hoped Daddy could understand that.

But he couldn't. He couldn't even believe it for the longest time. He walked around numb, note in hand, looking for Mother in all the closets of the house, inside the refrigerator, which he opened and closed a thousand times a day, in the attic, in his dresser drawers, in his unmade bed, in the trunk of the car. It was like it was a game she was playing and all he had to do was look in the right place and he would find her hiding there.

Days passed with Marty and Click asking, "Where's Mother? Where did she take Juan?"

"She's gone away for a while," Daddy said. "She'll be back soon."

I think our blood knew that was a lie, but we also suspected that such a lie was a far superior thing to the truth of the matter. I think it was our stomachs that knew that—the truth. The way our stomachs knotted and practically shut down. We could barely eat the holiday leftovers Daddy shoveled at us, nasty fruitcake, soggy divinity, chocolate-covered cherries, not to mention leftover ham with those smelly cloves in it and turkey that was so dried out we could hardly swallow it. Marty went to the bathroom almost all day every day. You could hardly walk by the bathroom door without seeing Marty sitting there on the toilet. "Close the door," I told him a thousand times. Mother leaving us, it just hollowed Marty out like a drum.

I don't know if we three would ever have understood what had happened if it hadn't been for Mrs. Ward coming by our house night after night, almost hysterical in her rage against Daddy. "How could you let this happen?" she asked him every night. Sometimes she tugged at the hair on her head so absentmindedly that it looked like she might yank it out by the fistfuls. Sometimes she started crying and could not stop and Daddy would pour her a glass of the leftover Christmas Mogan David wine and she would drink it even though she was mostly a religious person. Marty, Click, and I listened to every word Mrs. Ward spoke. We filed it under a huge imaginary file in our heads titled, *Things We Are Too Young to Have to Know*. I am proud to say that we didn't do a lot of crying or anything. Not even Click, as young as he was. Marty peed so much that there was nothing left in his body to be a tear. Me, I don't know why I didn't cry, because I was not ashamed to. I'd cried over many a lesser thing in my life. Unlike Marty and Click I didn't really have an aversion to crying. I'd been called a crybaby more times than I could count. But listening to Mrs. Ward sob and weep night after night, it just sort of dried me up that way. I guess you could say she did the crying for all of us. "How long do you think this has been going on?" she asked Daddy every night. "How long?"

It took Daddy a while to realize that we had caught drift of the story. Even then he refused to yield to the truth of the matter. "When will Mother be back?" Marty asked him daily.

"Before you know it," Daddy would say.

"You promise?" Marty said.

"Your mama loves you three too much to stay gone long," Daddy said. "She'll get to missing you so bad that she'll have to come home."

"You promise?" Marty kept on.

"Your mama is not about to miss watching you grow up," Daddy said. "Your mama loves you too much."

"Even more than Mike Ward?" Marty asked.

"Yes," Daddy said, "even more than that."

We went to sleep soothed by his lies night after night. It was better than warm milk and cookies for putting us to sleep. It was better than Pepto-Bismol, the bubblegum of medicines, to soothe our truth-sensing bellies.

The following months, Mrs. Ward kept us every day after school. It was terrible. We hated it so bad. Daddy said Mrs. Ward needed the money and it was the least he could do, pay her to watch us in the afternoons. Pay her for the fact that our mother had run off with her for-better-or-worse husband, her only viable means of support. Mike Ward — the man who used to take up the collection at church. The man who made Mother believe there was more to life than having babies, doing laundry, packing lunches, and watching *Price Is Right* and *Queen for a Day* on TV. The man who introduced her to the thrill of dictation and typing eighty-five words a minute.

We wished Daddy would just pay Mrs. Ward to leave us alone. No price seemed too high. We wanted to go home and watch cartoons at our own house after school, eat Popsicles and Fritos, play killing each other with our killing toys. We wanted to pinch, kick, call names, and scream at each other like we used to when we were normal. Before Mrs. Ward took all the fun out of what was left of our lives.

Mrs. Ward punished us for being Mother's children. We couldn't breathe at Mrs. Ward's house. Not even her own kids could breathe over there. All we did was try to hate them as much as they hated us. Try to make them stay away from us and stop saying whatever they were saying. And Mrs. Ward always took their sides too. Made us sit off by ourselves until we apologized — or else she called Daddy at work and told on us. "I'm really worried about your children, Edward," she said. "They aren't making a good adjustment at all."

For a short period I think Mrs. Ward got the idea that maybe she would have a romance with Daddy. That under the circumstances he might be her best bet for getting on with her life — and for getting even with Mike Ward and Mother wherever they were, off having a wonderful time. It wasn't that Mrs. Ward was ugly or anything. She looked okay. It's just that she didn't understand Daddy at all. She mistook his small gestures of concern for something else. Next thing we knew she was knocking on the door late at night again, but not to cry. She woke us up standing at the door in her see-through nightgown and housecoat. She had her hair pinned up. She smelled like sprayed-on honeysuckle. She wore lipstick. Daddy let her come in the first couple of times. He sent us back to bed but I heard him talking to her and I got up and looked where they were sitting in the kitchen, she in her flimsy gown and robe and Daddy in his pajama bottom with his hair standing on end. They whispered and Mrs. Ward put her hand on top of Daddy's. It wasn't until I interrupted them, saying, "My stomach hurts," and Mrs. Ward tried to nurse me back to bed with milk of magnesia, but I resisted, that she gave up and went home.

"What did she want?" I asked Daddy.

"She's lonely," he said. Then Daddy went back to bed and I did too. This happened more than once. Sometimes he met Mrs. Ward at the back door and hugged her and stuff. I saw them. Sometimes she spent the night with him and they locked his bedroom door and ignored me when I knocked on it and called Daddy's name over and over. I know he heard me.

When the bank foreclosed on Mrs. Ward's house—when Daddy let that happen the same way he had let Mother run off with Mrs. Ward's husband—then I think she finally gave up on

Daddy. She called him a bunch of names and said she hoped he rotted in hell. She loaded up her kids and they moved down to Gainesville, Florida, where Mrs. Ward's sister lives. She said her sister had married somebody who had made something of himself. We were jealous that they got to live in Florida, but Marty, Click, and I were never so happy to see any people move away in our lives. It was like we could breathe again.

On Click's birthday I made his cake myself. It was chocolate. It didn't turn out right so I had to just make it into the shape of a mountain with my bare hands and then pour the icing over it. I told him it was a volcano cake. He liked it. Daddy brought him a police hat, handcuffs, billy stick, and pistol. It was a complete law enforcement set. While Click was opening it Daddy said, "You'll never guess what I got at work today. A letter from your mother." We all three froze in place and looked at Daddy. "She sent you this birthday card right here," he handed Click a card with a clown on the front. "Look inside," Daddy said. "She put you five dollars in there."

Click stared at the five-dollar bill taped to the card. He read the words, "I love you," and saw where Mother had written her name. He took the card and went back to his room to study it in privacy. I think all three of us were suddenly struck with what an amazing and wonderful person our mother truly was. We were assured of her good-heartedness, which—under the circumstances—we had come to question. But Click's birthday card proved it. That she was a good woman after all. We were thrilled to know it.

That night Marty and me helped Daddy make supper. We had hotdogs and baked beans and potato chips. All Click's favorites. Afterwards we had volcano cake with seven candles stuck on the top so when we lit them the icing would melt and it'd look like the volcano was erupting.

"Make a wish, Click," Daddy said. "Go ahead, son."

"I already did," he said.

WITH MRS. WARD gone things began to look up a little. Daddy let me be in charge of keeping Marty and Click after school on a trial basis. There were rules. No neighborhood kids inside the house while Daddy was gone. Marty and Click had to play in our own yard, could not wander around the neighborhood bothering people like they used to. The rule was Daddy should never call home without my being able to lay my eyes on Marty and Click instantly. Their whereabouts were my primary responsibility— the new focus of my life. I should be able to call them to the phone at any moment without undergoing any sort of search. So I watched them like a hawk. I hovered over them like my life depended on it.

Also, I was not allowed to beat them up or hit them with anything. And they weren't supposed to hit me either, which was a joke. But since I couldn't get after them with Daddy's belt or the flyswatter or switches or anything the way Mother used to, I found a different way to make them act right. Food. If they wanted any, they had to get it from me and I wasn't giving it out unless they more or less minded what I said. It was amazing what a boy would do for a Moon Pie or a handful of fried pigskins. Overall it was a much better mess to be in than those afternoons at Mrs. Ward's house. None of us wanted to foul the thing up—for fear Daddy might pay somebody else to torture us the way Mrs. Ward had.

Most nights Daddy cooked our suppers. Or brought something home in a sack. Barbecue mostly and slaw. Sometimes fried chicken and biscuits. We didn't care what it was really, as long as there was plenty. He also brought bottles of liquor, gin and vodka mostly, in paper bags—even though before everything happened he didn't believe in drinking except on special occasions. Now he poured liquor into his sweet tea or Pepsi and sipped it while we told him about our day, trying to distract him from Mother's absence, which shrank the tiniest bit with each week that passed. Daddy kept his liquor in the cabinet above the refrigerator and we learned to check the bottles daily to see what frame of mind he was in. Those liquor bottles were like gauges to tell us how worried we needed to be.

When we sat down to supper, Daddy made one of us—usually me—ask the blessing and we mumbled through it like Mother used to make us do when she was here. Most nights we ate on paper plates and used paper cups so there was nothing much to clean up afterward. Within just the first few weeks Marty, Click, and I all learned the futility of telling on each other. Not because we had no tales to tell, but because we saw the way our tattling deflated Daddy, took the air out of him, caused him to slump at the supper table and put his head in his hands. He wanted us to be good. He needed that. So we embarked on an unspoken agreement to fake it.

Every night after supper, Daddy laid on the sofa like a man who'd been shot and might not live until morning. He drank his vodka from a paper cup and got mad if we horsed around and made him spill it. We sprawled near him on the floor, touching him — his foot, his arm, his chest — to be sure, hoping there was somebody on TV funny enough to make him laugh. It could be Lucy or Jack Benny or Red Skelton. We waited for them to deliver a joke the same way you wait for an ambulance. When Daddy laughed, when he barely chuckled, we did too. We howled like maniacs.

BY THE TIME the Christmas season rolled around again and Mother had been gone nearly a year we were pretty sure she wouldn't be coming back. She'd sent Daddy a birthday card to give to each of us on the proper day. Twice he told us that she'd called just to ask him how we were doing and he'd told her we were the best kids in the world and why didn't she come home and see for herself.

"Didn't you tell her we miss her?" I asked.

"I think she knows that," he said.

"Is she still coming back like you said?" Marty asked.

"She'll be back," Daddy assured us. "You'll see."

"When?" Marty asked.

"When she's ready," Daddy said. "When she can't stand it anymore."

DADDY'S MOTHER, OUR Grandmother Sue Mack, came to stay with us over Christmas holidays. It was nice because she cooked the best food ever, cleaned up everything, sewed buttons on things, darned the holes in socks, and played loud Christmas music on the hi-fi. She also took all our mother's clothes out of her closet and sorted them, some to give away, some to rip into dust rags. She didn't ask Daddy if it was okay, she just did it. Mother's slips, panties, and nightgowns too. Everything. We saw the box she'd set out to go to the Salvation Army. It made us feel like our mother had died. Like official word had come from a long distance. At night we'd hear Grandmother Sue Mack making dust rags out of mother's clothes too threadbare to give away. The ripping sound was so loud I put my pillow over my head and nearly smothered myself trying not to think about it.

"It's time," Grandmother Sue Mack said when she saw how stricken we looked at the sight of the Salvation Army box. "There might be somebody who can use these clothes."

"What if Mother comes home and wants her clothes back?" Marty asked.

It was a stupid question. Grandmother Sue Mack looked at him and said, "Well, if she comes home, I guess your Daddy will have to buy her some nice new clothes then."

That's all Marty really wanted to know—that our grandmother was willing to play along with us the game we were playing for as long as it took. Marty took one of Mother's sleeveless cotton shirts out of the Salvation Army box and took it to his room.

The week before Christmas Daddy and us put up the tree like always and plugged the plastic candles in the windows. Daddy wrote MERRY XMAS in the picture window with a can of fake snow. Like southern children everywhere we sang along with Bing Crosby, *I'm dreaming of a white Christmas,* an outright lie, so heartfelt. We cut snowflakes from sheets of white paper and taped them everywhere. We'd read in our schoolbooks about sleds, mittens, snowballs, and all manner of strange stuff. We were curious about these peculiar Yankee children—first Alice and Jerry, then Dick and Jane—but never jealous. We would not trade our warm Christmases for their cold ones. We slung strands of tinsel at the tree by the fistfuls and marveled at the sheer beauty of it—those metallic icicles thrilling us as much as any real ones could. Maybe more.

Our letters to Santa were low-key this particular Christmas, especially mine since by now I was ready to stop pretending. So was Marty. But we didn't want Click to have to give up until he was ready, so we all wrote out our Christmas lists like true believers. As usual Click wanted everything in the Sears Christmas catalog. Marty wanted a sleeping bag, a tent of his own, also maybe a hatchet and a gas lantern. There was no way they were getting all that. On the top of Marty's list though—like a preface to his own wishes—was a list that read, *For Daddy, Please bring: a color TV, a riding lawnmower, a pop-up camper, an electric guitar, a charcoal grill, a diamond ring.*

"Daddy doesn't want a diamond ring," I said when I saw his list.

"You don't know," Marty snatched his list from my line of sight. He'd gone through the catalog, like always, and circled the items he wanted, only this time he had also marked all the stuff he wanted Daddy to get for Christmas. It was about everything they had in there for men, except for socks and underwear. He'd also put two other items on his list. A little toy tractor for Juan. An electric mixer for Mother. Marty was never an ordinary boy. Marty was different from the start.

My list was simple. It said, *Dear Santa, No dolls please. Sincerely, Kendall.*

Grandmother Sue Mack hid our presents in the trunk of her car. We saw lots of them when she came home from the grocery store. At night we could hear her ripping Mother's clothes to shreds and wrestling with wrapping paper while she wrapped our gifts up and talked to Daddy about the future. She thought Daddy should come to his senses and stop waiting for Mother to come to hers. She thought we all should. "There are plenty of fish in the sea," she told him.

I knew everything we were getting for Christmas because at night I sneaked down the hall and spied on them. Daddy laid on the sofa in a holiday stupor sipping Mogan David wine until his lips were purple. Grandmother Sue Mack stitched patches on the knees of Marty's and Click's dungarees and talked Daddy's ears off giving him advice and encouragement on getting through the holidays—and life. "Do you guess she'll be in touch with the children on Christmas?" she asked Daddy. "Christmas is a time for children."

"No," he said.

"She remembered their birthdays."

"No she didn't," Daddy said. "She's been gone nearly a year now and there hasn't been any word from her at all. None."

"But the children said . . ."

"I know what they said."

ON CHRISTMAS MORNING Santa left us plenty of evidence that he was real. Including the clever disappearance of the Oreos we left out for him. After the frenzy had settled down some, Daddy, still wearing his pajama bottoms, sauntered casually over to the front door and opened it letting in a blast of chilly gray air. "What's this?" he asked, turning to look at the three of us huddled around our presents. "Somebody left some gifts out here on the step. Look."

Click made a dash for the door, but Marty and I just looked at each other. "Here," Daddy handed a present to Click, "looks like something for you. Well, what do you know," Daddy smiled, "it's from your mother. How about that?" Click ripped into the present on the spot. It was a dartboard and a set of darts. "Wow," Daddy said. "Look what your mama sent you, you two," he handed Marty and me presents with our names on them. An army canteen for Marty. A little jewelry box for me, the kind where the pink ballerina twirls on the top. "I guess your mother was thinking about you today," Daddy said. "I bet she wishes she was here with us on a day like this."

Grandmother Sue Mack made hot chocolate for everybody. She called me and Marty into the kitchen to help her carry it. She pulled our faces into her soft powdery bosom. "He lies because he loves you," she said.

"We know," Marty jerked away from her, sloshing hot chocolate all over the floor.

We had pancakes and country ham for breakfast. There was turkey roasting in the oven for later. The Christmas music was loud and cheerful. Daddy and Marty went outside to see if they could put up the pup tent Marty got for Christmas. Daddy took his paper cup with him. I helped Grandmother Sue Mack in the kitchen. She showed me how to make giblet gravy. She had broken my rule and given me a doll for Christmas but I wasn't mad. It was a small rag doll she had made herself out of our mother's leftover clothes. The doll's clothes were sewn right on to her body so they couldn't be removed. The hair was red yarn and the eyes were buttons. "Someday this might mean something to you," she told me.

I swore to myself I would not tear it up. Or let Marty and Click tear it up. I swore I would take care of it the best I could. I remember thinking at the time how fine it would be if ever Grandmother Sue Mack might run into our mother somewhere in this world just going about her business. Maybe she would mention to her in passing that she had given me something nice and I had sincerely appreciated it and taken good care of it. I bet my mother would be amazed to hear that. I liked to picture the surprised look on her face.

Largesse

by Gail Godwin

Christina had a rich aunt she had never met, her mother's first cousin, actually. Aunt Demaris lived on a ranch in Alabama part of the year and on a ranch in Texas the other part. She and her cattleman husband had not been blessed, as she put it, with children. Her Christmas presents to Christina, which usually arrived before Thanksgiving, were lavish and sometimes completely inappropriate. Christina was allowed to open them at once because her mother and grandmother were just as curious as she was to see what was inside.

One Christmas a sizeable box arrived from Maison Blanche in New Orleans. Excavating through postal paper, store gift wrapping, and tissue paper, all of which the grandmother folded and saved, they confronted what at first appeared to be some flattened exotic animal. But no, it was a child's coat of spotted fur with matching hat and muff.

"She's out of her mind," said Christina's mother, "this is *leopard* skin. And it's her handwriting on the card, so it's not some hired shopper's folly this time."

"The child can't possibly wear this to school," said the grand-mother. "And she certainly can't wear it to church."

"Perhaps they haven't heard at Maison Blanche or out at the ranches that there's a war on," remarked Christina's mother in the low deadpan voice she employed for her caustic mode.

They gave the coat, hat, and muff to the cleaning woman's little daughter. Christina's grandmother lied tactfully that the coat was too tight in the arms for Christina, and that of course the hat and muff must stay part of the ensemble. Christina never tried on the coat, nor did she remember wanting to. The thank-you note had to be written all the same, and she went to work on it on Christmas Day, after the presents had all been opened and there was a sad lull in the living room. Her grandmother was doing a crossword puzzle. The Christmas Day edition of the local news-paper rested on her mother's lap; she had been rereading the inter-views she had done with the wounded servicemen at the local military hospital.

"So far I've got *Dear Aunt Demaris*," Christina said glumly.

"That's an opener," said Christina's mother. "Be thankful I didn't name you Demaris."

"You wouldn't have!"

"She hinted. But I said your father had his heart set on Christina."

"He did?" Christina's father had been out of the picture since her infancy and she was always interested in more information about him when her mother was willing to volunteer it.

"No. He wanted to name you Greta."

"*Why?*"

"Oh, after Garbo. I don't know."

"*Dear Aunt Demaris. Thank you so much for the*—What? Help me!"

"You need an adjective," said her mother.

"I think I used *wonderful* last year."

"Let's see: *remarkable, unusual, unprecedented*..." Her mother uttered a snort and lost control. "Thank you so much for that unprecedented disaster of a coat." They both dissolved into wild laughter.

When they had finished, the grandmother, without looking up from her puzzle, suggested, "How about *grand*? Thank you so much for the grand coat."

"Mother, that's just inspired!" Christina's mother exclaimed in sincere admiration.

"I must get something out of my crosswords," replied the grandmother.

LIBERALITIES FROM THE unmet aunt in Texas marked successive Christmases: the filigree and pearl music box that played "Toora Loora Loora"; the gold mesh bracelet studded with heart-shaped diamond chips that Christina admired on her wrist until she lost it in midsummer; the brocaded kimono bathrobe with its big sleeves that caught on doorknobs; the rabbit fur jacket, worn once to a dance and then packed away. Christina's thank-you notes got easier, as did her command of adjectives most likely to impress and please. After Aunt Demaris requested it, she always enclosed a school picture of herself.

When Christina was fifteen, Aunt Demaris wrote, or rather her secretary wrote and Aunt Demaris signed the letter in her ornamented script, inviting Christina to spend Christmas with them at their Texas ranch. While the mother and grandmother were debating over what to do, a telegram arrived: ALL EXPENSES PAID OF COURSE STOP PHONE COLLECT STOP EAGER TO HEAR.

"Well, here it comes," said the grandmother.

"Pandora's box," Christina's mother enigmatically murmured. "What about it, Christina? It's your invitation. Would you like to go?"

"I don't know, I guess it would be an experience." Christina tried to picture how the older couple would go about entertaining her. She was pretty sure there would be shopping. She hoped her uncle would not expect her to ride a horse well.

The phone call was made, not collect, the mother and grandmother were too proud, but then they regretted it. First a maid who couldn't speak English answered and had to go and get another maid who could, and then Aunt Demaris was "detained" for a while longer. When at last her cousin came on the phone, Christina's mother's face crunched between the eyebrows and, looking strained, she started speaking in a funny way. At first it sounded like a parody of someone being gushy, but later she explained to Christina that Aunt Demaris brought that out in you.

After Christina's mother finished the phone call, she declared herself exhausted and went to lie down.

The airplane ticket arrived, followed by a huge package from Neiman Marcus. Inside was a white Samsonite suitcase and inside the suitcase were a black velvet skirt and top, a turquoise velvet cummerbund, a black taffeta slip, and dangling earrings of turquoise and hammered gold.

"I suppose she trusts us enough to supply the proper underclothes," the grandmother remarked as she carefully folded the tissue paper.

In the weeks preceding the trip, they crammed Christina with Demaris stories, some she'd heard before, but this time with an extra deliberateness, as though they were preparing her for some kind of test.

"She was always strong-willed," said the grandmother. "Even before her parents were killed. She was my husband's little niece. He and his brothers helped raise her in their mother's boarding house. This was when they were all struggling to make ends meet. The boys worked in the iron mines and came home every morning with rust-colored skin, and the mother cooked for the boarders and changed their sheets. But they treated Demaris like a princess, and I guess she just assumed that's what she was. When she was sixteen she made them all become Roman Catholics. All but my husband, he was in the Masons, you know, and had to refuse her. Then she met Karl, he was from a family of German immigrants, just a young assistant in a butcher shop. She made *him* become a Catholic and taught him math and good English and next thing you know they owned a meat market, and they branched out into cattle and before they knew it they were millionaires. Demaris credited their good fortune completely to the Lord, but she was always very appreciative of my husband's family. Though she never warmed to me. I was too reserved, I guess, the way mountain people are. And I wouldn't play cards with them on Sunday when we visited down in Alabama."

"I think the math and good English ought to get some credit for the fortune, too," said Christina's mother.

"Good English? I'm not so sure. Look at me and all *my* English—where has it gotten me?"

CHRISTINA'S MOTHER DROVE her a hundred and fifty miles across the state so that she could fly to Texas without having to change airplanes. This was possible because the junior college where she taught English for not enough money was on Christmas break. Despite her brilliant feature stories (what other local reporter could have interviewed Béla Bartók in French?) she had been let go from the newspaper after the war so that the men could have their jobs back. In her low moods, she could be quite caustic about this.

Christina's mother had turned down the grandmother's offer to come along. This made it into an adventure, since the two had never traveled anywhere alone. Mother and daughter left before dawn, while the stars were winking in the black winter sky. Aromas from the bacon and egg sandwiches and the thermos of coffee, packed by the grandmother, wafted enticingly from the backseat of the old car, bought new in a more prosperous era, when the grandmother's husband was alive. As they wound down the steep curves of the mountain roads and the sky began to lighten beyond the ranges, Christina's mother suddenly began to talk with a strange urgency about the father who had been out of the picture since her infancy. "He was just so damned handsome and charming and equally unsuitable, but I wanted him, and I got him. By the time you were on the way, I knew it wasn't going to work. But I still wanted you. Daddy was still alive and he and Mother wanted you, too."

"*Why* did you know it wasn't going to work?"

"He was unstable. Also he drank. When he was doing that he could be mighty cruel."

"You mean like *hit* you?"

"Oh, that, too, but the things he said hurt more."

"Like *what?*"

"I've forgotten. I really have. I need my self-esteem. And he was a sick person, so it wasn't entirely his fault. He was in a mental hospital for servicemen during the war."

"Is he . . . in one now?"

"No, the last I heard he was in Florida, teaching tennis in a hotel."

"Doesn't he ever want to see me?"

"I think he probably does, but, you know, Christina, everyone isn't as *resolute* as we are. Some people can want to do things, but then they don't follow through. Now your Aunt Demaris is the very opposite of your father. She follows through. Which is why I got onto this subject, which isn't my favorite. But I needed to fill you in some before you were exposed to . . . well, other points of view." She was being unusually careful in choosing her words. "When Daddy died suddenly, Demaris and Karl drove up for the funeral in their Cadillac and we'd hardly buried him before Demaris made me a proposition. She wanted me to bring you to live with them, she wanted to sort of adopt us both. The offer didn't include Mother. Demaris didn't like Mother very much. She considered her 'cold'—Mother didn't know how to gush—and also I think Demaris had Mother's role in mind for herself. I said I would need some time to consider it."

"Did you consider it?"

"Not really. Oh, I fantasized some. Obviously we would have been spoiled to death, but I would have sacrificed our independence. And how could I have just deserted my own mother like that at such a time? But Demaris is the type of person it's easier to turn down in a letter."

They were down the mountain curves. The morning sun grew stronger along the straight road until they could feel its heat inside the car. "Why, it's plain warm down here in the flatlands!" said Christina's mother. She pulled into a roadside picnic area and they ate their sandwiches in their coats at a table strewn with fallen leaves and acorn shells. Each time they unscrewed the top of the thermos, the hot coffee sent steam into their cold faces. "Well, isn't this just *grand*," declared her mother meaningfully, and they both recalled the leopard coat and hat and muff and burst into giggles. The mother breathed in the sharp, clean air and looked around with delight at the deserted picnic grounds and the bare trees. "You know, despite everything, I am glad to have kept my independence. I hope you will feel I did right."

THE ELDERLY MAN by the window offered to trade places with her when he learned that this was to be Christina's first flight. They changed seats and he laughed good-naturedly when he had to keep letting out the seatbelt straps to make ends meet over his portly middle. He sat back in complacent nonchalance as the plane roared and shuddered and raced down the runway past the point of no return and lifted into an emptiness tilting dangerously to one side and then the other. Christina was grateful to have the example of his calm masculine demeanor. By the time they reached cruising altitude, the most amazing fictions, replete with realistic details, were pouring out of her in response to his congenial inquiries. She was going to spend Christmas with her father, who owned ranches in Texas and Alabama. Yes, her mother and father were divorced, had been since she was a little baby. At first they had been crazy about each other, but it just didn't work out.

That happens, he said with an understanding nod.

Her father insisted on having her every other Christmas. They would ride around the ranch on horseback and then go into town and have lunch and go shopping. Her mother always worried he would spoil her with all his money, but she had hopes and dreams of her own, and besides, she valued her independence.

As they were landing, the man declared feelingly that he would have considered himself honored by the gods to have been granted a smart, lovely daughter like her.

As they disembarked, an elegant, sharp-faced man in black tie and evening clothes stepped forward at the gate and pronounced her name. For an instant she was confused, it was like walking into her own fantasy. As the man was introducing himself as Clint, who worked for her uncle, she was aware that her traveling companion, a few passengers behind, would assume he was witnessing the father-daughter reunion. What if he should come up to them and say something to expose her? But he passed on discreetly, with a brief nod and a wistful smile.

Close up, Mr. Clint, as he told Christina everyone called him, was not as elegant as his first impression. His face was tough and large-pored, and after he had stored her suitcase in the trunk of the Cadillac and explained that her aunt and uncle were at a dinner party they couldn't get out of and had sent him to meet her, settle her in at the house, and then go back to pick them up, she decided he must be some kind of upper-grade servant, between a butler and a chauffeur. But he was a smooth-enough talker without saying or asking much and glibly kept awkwardness at bay.

It was dark by the time they turned into the gates of the ranch, which was named "New Canaan" on Aunt Demaris's stationery, so she couldn't admire the approach, which Mr. Clint boasted was stunning. In daylight from this entrance road you could see a hundred miles in both directions. That would be farther than she and her mother had driven today. But it would be a hundred miles *less* than her mother would have driven on the round trip. For some reason this gave Christina satisfaction.

The house was lit as though the aunt and uncle were having a huge party themselves, but inside there was nobody at home but the maids in their black uniforms and white aprons, only one of whom spoke so-so English. They served Christina her lone supper in the chandeliered dining room: thin slices of steak in a tasty sauce, with yellow rice and some spicy compote and warm tortillas swaddled in white linen on a silver dish, with guacamole and sour cream and a pale-green relish heaped attractively in crystal side dishes. She would probably have eaten twice as much if they hadn't been taking turns peeking at her through the tiny hole in the kitchen door. She tried a bite of the mystery relish and choked: she had drunk all the water in her goblet. The maid who didn't speak English burst through the swinging door with a pitcher of water. "Too *caliente*," Christina apologized between gulps. "But it's *muy buena, gracias.* Everything is just *muy buena! La comida es mucha buena.*"

The other maid rushed into the dining room. Standing on either side of her they began chattering eagerly at her in their language.

Christina exhausted her meager supply of Spanish phrases convincing them she could not follow. For dessert there was flan with caramel sauce, and a small glass of a sweet pinkish wine.

Big and little clocks, distant and close, kept chiming the quarter hours and still they didn't come. Christina felt it would show poor manners to go to her room and lie down, so she chose a tolerably comfortable straight-backed brocade sofa, beneath a life-size oil painting of a platinum blond Rubenesque lady in a low-cut red gown and red jewels. Feeling more relaxed from the sweet wine, she arranged herself into a portrait of a modest young woman awaiting, not at all resentfully, the return of two *grand* people she had been longing to meet. The Christmas tree in the corner of the living room was loaded with ornaments that had the look of all being bought at the same time. It was bigger and bushier than the one that now took up most of their living room back home, but this room was big enough to dwarf the larger tree. Beneath the tree were piled dozens of professionally wrapped presents, an excessive number of them bearing cards with her name. She wished she had brought gifts, but nobody had been able to come up with any sure idea of what might please the millionaire relatives.

The Texas Christmas tree blinked its colored lights at her. On and off. On and off. They will be getting ready for bed now at home, Christina thought. My grandmother is switching off her last program; my mother reads a couple more paragraphs in her library novel, then sighs and turns down the page. Maybe they are speaking of me at this very moment. Then with a desolate jolt she remembered they were two time zones later than she and by now would be asleep. On and off blinked the lights.

Then there was a sudden brightness and energy, a burst of outdoor air and a fusillade of extravagant welcomes and endearments. The maids fluttered about like two nervous blackbirds, plucking at the sleek coats of the two large people who stood quite sumptuously still, allowing themselves to be unwrapped for her delight. Christina heard herself called blessed girl and darling one and *much* prettier than her pictures and a great deal more. She was praised exorbitantly for her courtesy in waiting up for them. Now she, too, was standing, offering herself to their hugs and compliments and perfumed kisses. Aunt Demaris was of course the platinum blond lady in the oil painting, only now she was wearing a black gown and different jewels and had grown much more Rubenesque in figure. But her face was still elegantly planed and beautiful. "We had a *flat tire,* of all things! Would you believe it, darling?"

"Inexcusable is what I say," roared the big rosy uncle. "A brand new automobile just out of the showroom and there we are on the side of a dirt road, me and Mr. Clint, jacking up a blowout in our tuxedos." Despite the mishap, he seemed elated.

"He was superb, Christina. Yes, you were, my darling. Mr. Clint wasn't too keen on spoiling *his* finery until your Uncle Karl here set the example. He gave me his cuff links to hold and rolled up his sleeves and got right down to business in the dirt."

"I hope I haven't forgotten how to change a tire," said the uncle, whose clothes bore no sign of any contact with the dirt. "Well, well, well, Demmie," he exclaimed expansively, an arm around each of them. "We hit the jackpot, didn't we, with this pretty girl here!"

AFTER ANOTHER GLASS of the sweet wine for her and her aunt, and "something stronger" for the uncle, during which there were extensive inquiries about her airplane flight and her dinner and the well-being of her mother and grandmother, whom Aunt Demaris said they must remember to phone first thing in the morning, they sent Christina off to bed. Since she had been to her room last, the maids had unpacked her new suitcase and put everything away where they thought it should go and turned off some lamps and turned on others. Everything looked inviting and pretty, if a little stuffy and overdone. Her folded pajamas awaited her on the pillow, her cosmetics and brush and comb were laid out across the glass top of the vanity. She hung up her dress and got into her pajamas and went into the adjoining bathroom to rinse out her stockings and panties. She had just arranged them on the towel rack above the bathtub and was drying off her hands when there was a soft knock at the bedroom door.

"I simply had to see my girl one more time," said her aunt, sweeping in. "Ah, you're already in your dear pajamas. Are these flannel? We might want to get you something lighter while you're in Texas." Demaris had changed into a creamy satin kimono with braided gold loops down the bosom. Her face, cleaned of its makeup and lubricated for the night with an orange-smelling cream, made her seem simpler and more open.

"Come sit here by me on the bed and let me look at you." Which she proceeded to do in minuscule detail. Face, hair, nose, eyes, figure, were described and praised in turn. Then she stroked Christina's hands and pulled at the corners, proclaiming them to be exact replicas of her grandfather's. "Uncle Tommy had the same sweet hands, small for a man's, but strong—he worked in the iron mines when he was young, you know. He was the world's kindest man. I wish you could have known him!"

Christina said she wished she could have, too, adding that her mother and grandmother still spoke of him most every day.

"Not a *single* day goes by that *I* don't think of him," rejoined her aunt passionately, making Christina feel she had betrayed them at home by not exaggerating and saying every single day.

Aunt Demaris strolled into Christina's bathroom and stood gazing pensively down into the toilet bowl, as if hoping to read clues to her niece's character. Thank God she had flushed. Then she saw her aunt stiffen when she discovered the stockings and panties dripping on the towel rack above the tub. "Ah, darling," she scolded sadly. "We can't have you doing the *washing* here. We'll let it go this time, but from now on just put your little things in this net bag behind the bathroom door and Marta will take care of them for you."

CHRISTINA HAD NOT failed to notice the baby blue rosary draped invitingly across the small, framed wedding picture on her bedside table. A young, slim, rather fierce-looking bride clung proudly to the arm of her butcher boy husband. As it happened, Christina was acquainted with the mysteries of the rosary, as well as its soporific effects. But she had no desire to disturb it from its ornamental function tonight and presently consigned the whole room and its contents, as well as those of the adjoining bathroom, into pitch darkness. She arranged her limbs straight as a mummy's between the soft Marta-laundered sheets and simply breathed in and out until she could feel the return of her own spirit come like a sudden rush of oxygen to her lungs. Scenes she had no control of, based on nothing she had seen during this eventful day, surged toward her on the inside of her eyelids, then rapidly gave way to other scenes. As she lay there calming down she rightly guessed that she would make many stupid mistakes before the end of her visit, and that she would be forgiven each time, perhaps even loved more for them. They would be discussed as touching and charming and a little sad after she was gone.

Already she knew deep down in a part of herself she had yet to meet, that these people were not for her. But there would be future opportunities for temptation, and one or two times just short of desperation, when she would do her level best to surrender herself into their captive embrace. But each time, by the grace of God, wherever he operates from, and thanks to the independence her mother had early ruined her with, she would sabotage herself and blight her chances, again and again, with these grand people so eager to make life easy for her.

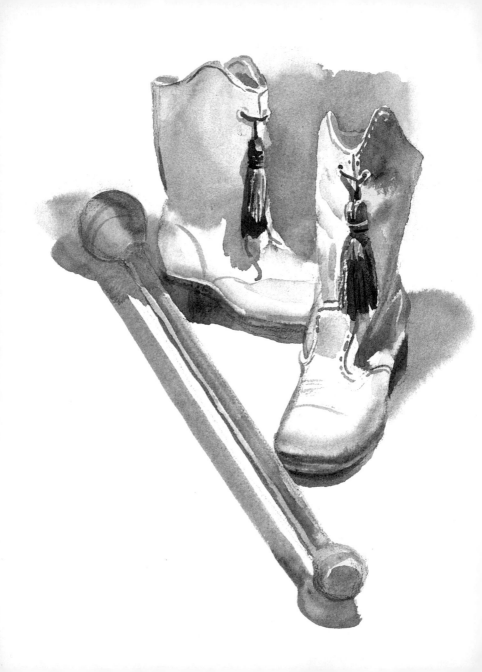

The Blue Carcoat

by Jill McCorkle

The Christmas parade of Fulton did not physically amount to much, usually just a few flatbed tobacco trailers that had been decorated by local service clubs with cotton snow and elves; sometimes high school girls stood poised, waving the stiff formal wave of beauty queens while the tobacco beds rocked and swayed beneath them. There were usually a few Shriners scattered about on mopeds, their horns and whistles blowing, and of course the high school band was in full force, the majorettes drawing wolf whistles from the high school boys who sat on parked cars and smoked cigarettes.

All of this took place year after year, the band and majorettes and floats all wedged between a police car with siren going and Santa bringing up the rear. Santa was usually perched on the back of a Volkswagen convertible made to look like a sleigh, cardboard reindeer strapped to the hood. The parade of 1972 was the same. Mama and I stood in front of a store called Foxy Mama, which specialized in Afro wigs. Misty was supposed to meet me there, and I kept scanning the crowd for her orange hair while the band approached. I liked the way the steady beat of the drums seemed to make my heart beat louder and faster. As the parade got closer, I was torn between wanting to grip my mother's arm in excitement and wanting to walk three blocks down so as not to be identified with her.

I saw across the street a souped-up red GTO, its owner stretched out on the hood with some other boys as he waited for her, his girl, that blond majorette, to march his way. If I turned to the side, I could see my reflection in the window of Foxy Mama, my hair much too curly for the shag haircut I had gotten. I willed my hair to look like Perry Loomis's, all one length and with flaxen waves like a princess. "What's so great about Perry anyway?" one of the girls in my class had asked in the bathroom one day. She was one of Ruthie Sands's friends, one of the few in that group who had not gone to private school when we integrated. "I just don't see why all the boys like *her.*" She looked around, her light hair filling with electricity as she brushed. Six of us stood there in front of the dark wavy mirrors, the old bathroom cold and smelling of rusty radiator heat and various mixtures of cologne. The graffiti on the walls dated back at least twenty years.

"I know why," Misty said, winking at me. Lately, she had been trying her best to attract interest in the two of us and what she called our "knowledge of the world."

"Because she's new," I said, giving my contribution to the conversation in a way that seemed too well rehearsed yet still carried no impact at all.

"Nope." Misty slung her arm around my shoulder and squeezed.

"It's because she puts out." I felt my face redden as the other girls stepped closer. Misty had them, these Ruthie Sands groupies, right where she wanted them. "Todd Bridger has all but *done the deed* with her." I knew Misty was quoting what Dean, *Mister Maturity*, had told her; she was nodding, mouth stretched in a knowing grimace. Her words left me feeling odd as if my insides had been twisted, and I forced the same nervous laughter that came from the other girls, so as not to show my embarrassment; or was it envy? I felt as if they had all seen right into my head—seen the way I had strutted across my mind in that fake-fur coat, like maybe I was Ann-Margret on my way to meet Elvis, seen the way I had kissed Todd Bridger or some faceless, nameless boyfriend in the back of the Cape Fear theater, and then taken his hand and pressed it to my chest. I had imagined I was there in the red GTO as that high school senior inched his hand over to the majorette's thigh; imagined that I looked just like Perry, that I *was* Perry Loomis.

"Well, what did he do exactly?" Lisa Burke asked in her high little-girl voice.

"Use your brain now," Misty said and crooked her finger to give a hint. "Kate knows." She patted me on the shoulder and again gave me the look that meant *lift your chin*. "Kate and I know a lot."

WHEN MISTY FINALLY got to the parade, she whispered that she was late because she had stopped by Lisa Burke's house to loan her a copy of *Valley of the Dolls*. She assured me that I could read it next, and then she launched into her latest discovery, which was that Perry Loomis had to wear turtlenecks a couple of weeks ago because that older boyfriend of hers gave hickeys like mosquito bites. My mother and Mrs. Edith Turner turned and stared at Misty. Misty smiled sweetly, and then when Mrs. Turner wasn't looking, shot her the bird. The band was in front of us, and I felt my heart quicken as I watched the majorette and the boy on the GTO exchange looks, then a wink, lips puckered.

"The downtown has gone to pot," Mrs. Turner screamed, and pulled her mauve tunic close around her. "I don't know how on earth they stay in business." She pointed to the Afro wigs on display, her head shaking back and forth. She had the habit of constantly removing her glasses and letting them swing on the rhinestone-flecked chain around her neck while she cleaned the lenses again and again with a little wadded-up piece of tissue, a nervous habit, I suspected, for she had already confessed to being "scared of the coloreds," her fear being that "they are taking over the town; give them an inch and they'll take a mile." My father called Edith Turner *the paranoid image of Theresa Poole.* Fortunately, the parade was too crowded for Mrs. Poole's Adirondack, and instead she sat up in the manager's office in Woolworth and looked to the street below.

"What's it like at the schoolhouse? Hmmmm? Problems with them?" I realized that she was talking to me. "I said I bet they cause trouble there at the schoolhouse, taking over, using double negatives." I just stared at her not knowing what to say. "I do declare if your face hasn't improved. I would swear that place has gotten smaller or paler or something." She looked at my mother and nodded and then continued without even taking a breath. "And those children from out in the country"— she cleaned her lenses, peeked through, and then cleaned them again—"bad. I hear they are so bad. The filthy language. Filth."

"It's bad, the language is awful, just awful," Misty said, and nudged me right as Todd Bridger and some of the other boys from our class stepped into the crowd on the other side of the street. I kept losing sight of him while Mrs. Turner and my mother discussed how important it was to line a commode seat with toilet paper before sitting on it. Mrs. Turner said it was especially important at places like the movie theaters where they no longer had a separate bathroom for the *coloreds.*

"Is she stupid or what?" Misty asked, and then she was waving and calling out to Dean, who was on the other side of the street. I just stared straight ahead, concentrating on the huge bare tree limbs and the bright blue sky, and the little stone man down at the end of the block where the parade would circle onto the next street. The crisp wind stung my face and gave me a good excuse to put my gloves against my cheeks. "The language is *filthy*," Misty whispered in mimic. "What a stupid old bitch."

I saw Perry Loomis like a flash over the other side of the street, and it was like she was looking right at me. One day I had said hello to her in the hall, and she had looked surprised, as if to ask who did I think I was speaking to her. She had quickly nodded and then hurried past, her books up to her chest. Now I saw her face in and out of the crowd, the boys from my class not far from where she was. I looked past the float with what was *supposed* to look like the nativity but instead looked like some hippies in a barnyard; I had decided that I *would* speak to Perry again if I got the chance, even with Misty right there beside me. The high school drama students who were manning the float had *live* animals, and now Joseph had thrown down his walking stick and was wrestling a sheep who was butting the chicken wire that enclosed the flatbed trailer.

Once the animals were under control, and Santa finally passed, the crowd thinned. Children ran through an alley to catch the parade going back the other way. Again I saw Perry, now turning away from the curb and walking toward the corner. She was wearing a light blue carcoat that for the world looked like the one I had outgrown, and she had a little baby propped up on her hip like a grocery bag. I had once overheard Todd Bridger say that Perry's mama was never at home and they could do as they pleased as long as Perry cooked supper and changed her little brother's diaper. I lifted my hand when I thought she was looking but instead I got the same blank stare she had given me in the hall that day. Todd and some of the other boys were standing around her, but she seemed uninterested as she shifted the child from hip to hip, turning to smile as if she were paying attention to what they were saying, though she looked as if her thoughts were miles and miles away. It hardly seemed fair that anyone should be so pretty, with such thick wavy hair and large dark eyes.

IT WAS A relief for Christmas to come and go. Misty spent most of the days comparing that year to the one before. It was warmer than usual that Christmas and rained so much that the families who usually went all out with lights and decorations confined their efforts to the insides of their houses. "Thank God, they're not stringing their lights this year," Mama said, and pointed to the neighborhood behind us, Merle Huck's house dark. "There would be an electrical fire for sure."

NOT LONG AFTER we returned to school, I got my chance to talk to Perry. I had gotten permission to leave gym class to go to the bathroom, and there she was, sitting up on the old radiator with her hands cupping her chin as she rested against the large windowsill. The light blue carcoat was draped over her legs. She turned when she heard me come in and then quickly looked back to the schoolyard where a group of guys were shooting marbles under one of the tall elms.

"Hi," I said, pausing in front of the mirror to brush my hair. I saw her then turn and study my reflection, her lips in full pout. She nodded. I hesitated, trying to think of something, *anything* to say. "You're not sick, are you?" She shook her head, dabbed one eye with the sleeve of her coat, and then turned back to the window.

"I used to have a coat like that," I offered, hoping for a bit more conversation. I turned from the mirror and waited to see if she would respond.

"You mean you used to have this one." She shook the sleeve all bunched up in her tiny hand. Somehow I was not prepared for the twang of her voice, the rusty flatness that went against every smooth line of her face. The sound was coarse and grainy. "I don't care," she persisted, her eyes as hard and cold as creek pebbles. "You can have it back if you want it. It's got a rip in the lining. The pockets hadn't even been cleaned out; I found all kinds of little notes." She paused and then laughed a forced laugh. "Take it if you want it." She hopped down and stepped closer to me, the coat held out in front of her. I felt like I was in the bottom of a well, like when I used to wear my earplugs. The image of myself in the white fake fur was ugly and garish; I was ugly and garish, and I was prepared to hear her say it.

"I don't want it," I whispered. If Misty had been there, she would have been forcing my head up. "I'm sorry, really." I wanted to tell her that I didn't know, didn't think, but I knew if I said another word I'd start crying. I looked back at her, tried to show in my expression that I hadn't meant to hurt her. She returned my stare, her eyes lingering just a second longer on my left cheek, and I waited for what was bound to come, waited for the lengthy, flattened insult.

"Who needs a stupid new coat?" she said and turned away. "All of y'all come in here like a fashion show." She flipped one hand out to the side and twisted her small body in mocked exaggeration of a model pose. "And I've heard the things that fat friend of yours has said about me. I ain't deaf, you know, but it seems I can't do nothing about it." I froze, waiting for more, still stunned that she had concocted her *y'all* to include me. I was one of *them;* I was one of the enemy and she had not even taken her best shot at me. She sighed and went back to the radiator, hopped up and pulled her short corduroy skirt down as far as she could.

"I'm sorry," I said. She shrugged without looking from the window, and I backed out of the bathroom as quietly as I could. I was back in the gym, feeling the vibrations of the basketballs bouncing up and down the old scuffed-up floor, when I realized that I had not even used the bathroom. And when the bell rang, I lingered, looking out the gymnasium door to where Perry stood on the curb in front of the school until she climbed into an old beat-up van and rode away. The van, blue with all kinds of spray-painted graffiti, was easily recognized; I had seen it parked at the Huckses' house from time to time. The gym was almost empty when I heard Misty's loud, boisterous voice calling for me to come on, we were going to be late for English. *I ain't deaf you know.* We were doing the first act of *The Miracle Worker,* and I had Misty's old granny glasses safely tucked away in my locker.

SLOWLY THE LEAVES returned, green buds that soon opened like fans to camouflage the stone man so important to the annual Christmas parade, so that only those familiar with him would be able to trace his figure there against the sky. With spring, we received news that E. A. Poe High was close enough to completion that we would definitely go there in the fall; as a result, Samuel T. Saxon would finally be torn down. They would begin as soon as school got out, slowly dismantling the ancient mortar and brick, the thick wavy windows and stone sidewalks. They would bulldoze the yard, turning up lost erasers and marbles and pennies and burying them beneath the yellow dust.

Ponies for Christmas

by Michael Knight

It was nearly dark by the time Frank Posey arrived at his brother's house. He was spending Christmas in Middleburg with his brother, Ted, and his brother's wife, Marcy, and the twin girls, Jane Margaret and Colleen, five years old, born nineteen minutes apart. The whole family met him in the front yard, and Marcy put the twins through their paces—Remember Uncle Frank? Hello, Uncle Frank—then released them into the house. The grown-ups milled around a minute longer. As they were walking toward the door, frozen snow crunching underfoot, Ted briefed Frank on the home improvements they had made.

"We'll show you pictures," he said.

Marcy said, "You won't believe the difference."

The house itself—two-story colonial, red brick, white trim—had been the weekend retreat of a Nevada congressman who'd come up on the wrong end of a fund-raising scandal, and Ted, flush with a recent success in some tobacco litigation, had snatched the old place for half what it was worth. They started remodeling right away, Ted said, raising ceilings, knocking out walls, until the house was hard to recognize.

"It must have been pretty run down," Frank said.

They were in a guest room now, the last stop on the abbreviated tour. Ted had Frank's duffel bag in his right hand, an unlit cigar in his left. Marcy fluffed the pillows on Frank's bed. A row of windows looked out on a stretch of river. At low tide, the banks were icy and exposed, the water dark against the snowy lawn.

"No," Marcy said, "it was lovely."

Ted slipped his arm around her waist.

He said, "We just needed to make a little change."

They held the pose a moment, as if waiting for Frank to take their picture, before they moved apart.

For dinner, Marcy served she-crab soup and goat cheese salad followed by Virginia ham with English peas. The twins were fidgety and shy so Marcy let them carry their plates into the den, where they could watch TV. Marcy asked Frank about work (he designed ads for a Richmond weekly), and he asked her about motherhood. Ted went on about refurbishment. When the dishes had been cleared, Marcy and the twins retired to the master bedroom to wrap Ted's presents, and Frank found himself on the new sunporch in the new Jacuzzi with his older brother, nursing a glass of his brother's famous eggnog. Ted guarded the recipe like it contained illegal ingredients and he'd be put away for life if his secret were revealed.

"They're not beams," he said, responding to a compliment Frank had paid the renovations. "You call that a coffered ceiling. Purely ornamental nowadays. No support function whatsoever."

He was chest deep in scalding bubbles, his elbows propped on deck, limp-wristed. Frank was perched on the rim in a borrowed swimsuit with his ankles in the water.

"Is that right?" he said.

Ted launched into a history of coffered ceilings — popular in the Renaissance and in English manor houses, not found in colonial America, made a comeback just before the turn of the century — but Frank tuned him out. He shut his eyes. His fingertips were tingling faintly and he could feel his pulse in the softs of his elbows and the backs of his knees. He had the queasy feeling that time itself was bogging down. He heard his brother say something about pubic hair and opened his eyes again.

"What's that?"

"What's what?"

"You said something about pubic hair."

"I'm saying she didn't have any." Ted wiggled his eyebrows and clipped his tongue between his teeth.

"Marcy doesn't have pubic hair?" Frank said.

Ted made a sour face. "Of course Marcy has pubic hair. You don't *marry* a woman with no pubic hair. You don't let a woman with no pubic hair raise your *children.*"

"Then who doesn't have pubic hair?" Frank said.

"Heather *Trout,*" he said.

"You cheated on Marcy?"

Ted sighed and swiveled to look over his right shoulder as if there was a team of experts against the wall and he needed a second opinion on his little brother.

"Don't be stupid," he said. "I'm talking about college. I'm talking about Heather Trout. Haven't you been listening? You must've heard this story a hundred times."

"Sorry," Frank said.

"What's wrong with you?"

"Nothing," Frank said. "Tell the story."

"It's ruined," Ted said.

He peered into his drink. Frank stirred the Jacuzzi with his feet. Then Ted lifted his eyes and said, "Lemme have your glass."

"I'm all set," Frank said.

"Oh, no," Ted said, hopping out of the Jacuzzi. "This is Ted's famous eggnog. This is a Christmas tradition. I don't make this eggnog every day." He carried their glasses to the bar, leaving a trail of wet footprints, and refilled the drinks from a sweating pitcher. "So here's the plan," he said. "In the morning, we open presents and do a light breakfast, muffins and fruit or something, then church, then me and Marcy and the girls are headed over to Marcy's parents' house for lunch. You're welcome to come with us or else you can just knock around here till we get back. I thought maybe in the afternoon you and I could chip a few balls into the river."

"I should probably take off after breakfast," Frank said.

"You're kidding?" Ted said. "You drive three hours to spend one night? Don't be stupid. Hang around a couple days. Marcy thought you'd at least be here till Monday. She went shopping. She bought those cookies that you like—those Mallomars or whatever."

"I don't like Mallomars," Frank said.

Ted frowned and drew a breath and shouted, "Marrrrcy—"

"Don't come back here." Marcy's voice came from the bedroom. "You better not come back here."

Ted shouted, "What do you call those cookies Frank likes?"

"S'mores," she said.

Ted said, "S'mores."

"I do like S'mores," Frank said.

"Then it's settled," Ted said. "You'll stay until we're out of S'mores."

He came back around the bar and handed Frank his drink. He stomped his foot.

"Cashmere slate," he said. "From India. We went crazy. We re-did everything. We couldn't stop ourselves."

"It looks great," Frank said.

"Be right back," Ted said.

When he was gone, Frank stood and walked over to the French doors. The glass was fogged and he wiped the condensation with his wrist, but it was too dark to make out the river. He could see the patio—gas grill, picnic table, icicles hanging from the pergola—but that was all.

"All right," Ted said, returning with a pair of fat cigars. "We're in business." He sunk his body into the Jacuzzi and sighed. "Now, *this* makes me happy. My little brother is in town. My wife and daughters are in the next room wrapping Christmas presents. I have a fistful of cigars." He shook his head like he couldn't believe his luck.

"You talk to Dad?" Frank said.

Ted narrowed his eyes. He whipped one cigar at Frank, poked the other between his teeth.

"Last week," he said. "He wouldn't come."

"He say why not?"

"He's an asshole," Ted said. "That's why not. He didn't even come when the girls were born." Ted chewed the end of his cigar. "Why'd you have to bring him up? Now you've got me in a mood." He struck a match, puffed on his cigar until it lit, then tossed the book to Frank. Blue smoke hovered around his head. "What's the matter with you?" he said.

Right then, Marcy shepherded the twins into the room. They were big-eyed, like their mother, and wispy blond, like their mother, and round with baby fat. Marcy was slender as a flute. The twins had on matching white nightgowns and red ribbons in their hair. Frank could never tell which was which.

"The girls want a kiss goodnight," Marcy said.

She patted their behinds, and they shuffled over to Ted and hugged his neck and smacked their lips against his cheek.

Ted said, "Tell your Uncle Frank what you want for Christmas."

"A pony," they said in unison.

"I keep telling them a pony will just knock over the furniture and leave road apples on the rug."

"It won't live in the house," they said.

"Where will it live?" Frank said.

"In the yard," they said.

"All right," Marcy said. "Santa won't come unless you're both asleep."

"In separate beds," Ted said. He craned his neck to watch them leave. "I'm gonna come check in a little while and I want everybody in her own bed." When their footsteps had faded, he looked at Frank. In a quiet voice, he said, "They're real attached."

BY MIDNIGHT, THEY had fixed matching training wheels to matching kid-sized bikes, assembled matching doll houses and matching miniature kitchenettes and arranged everything around the tree. Marcy showed Frank before and after pictures of the house. Ted expounded on plaster work and real Brazilian cherry molding. They finished the pitcher of eggnog, and Ted revealed, while whipping up a second batch, that his secret ingredient was chili powder, though Frank suspected he was lying to throw him off the scent. Ted wanted to show Frank the ponies—there were two of them—who were bunking down the street in a neighbor's barn. Over Marcy's protests, they bundled into winter coats and hiking boots and followed a flashlight beam into the darkness. Marcy insisted that neither of them was in any condition to get behind the wheel.

"I bought a barn for our place," Ted said, his words misting on the air. "This great old thing Marcy found up in Vermont. What they do is tear it down and number the boards, then piece it back together here. We'll put it by the river. Fence off a pasture and build a riding ring back there. We have to wait till after Christmas, of course, so the girls will be surprised."

"How many acres do you have?" Frank said.

"Twelve and change," Ted said. "Eight hundred feet of waterfront."

"Nice," Frank said.

They walked down a hill in the middle of the road. There was no traffic, no sound except their voices, no artificial illumination except the flashlight beam. The road was icy in patches, and Frank lost his footing and clutched his brother's sleeve for balance.

Ted said, "I can't believe you don't remember Heather Trout."

"The girl with no pubic hair?"

"That's her," Ted said. He stopped in his tracks, shook his head, then moved forward again. "I mean every third woman probably shaves her bush these days, but back then—back in college—you just didn't hear about that kind of thing."

"I don't think it's that common," Frank said.

They came up beside a split-rail fence. Another fifty yards and Ted veered left down a pea-gravel drive. He swung the light against the side of an immense white house.

"You call that Greek Revival," he said.

He led Frank between a row of boxwoods, through a gate and across a pasture to the barn. The barn smelled pleasantly musty— wood and hay and horse tack. Horses nickered in their stalls. A bay with a braided mane stuck its head out to look them over. At the last stall on the left, Ted stopped and aimed the light inside. Two black ponies wearing identical red bridles gazed back at them.

"The good thing about Hilton ponies," Ted said, "is they don't look like midget horses. You know how Shetlands are all fat and stumpy. These guys have the right proportions."

"They look like dolls," Frank said.

Their eyes were glassy and reflective, their tails neatly bobbed. Frank lowered himself onto a wooden bench.

Ted said, "A thousand bucks apiece and in a week the girls will only be riding one of them. That's what they do. They want to sleep in the same bed, eat off the same plate, share the tub. They *talk* at the same time. Have you noticed that? It's creepy. Marcy thinks it's no big deal. But it doesn't sit with me. They ought to be more independent."

"They're just kids," Frank said.

Ted shined the light on Frank.

"What's your problem?" he said.

"Nothing," Frank said.

Ted sighed and sat beside him and thrust his feet out and crossed his arms in what struck Frank as a posture of resignation, though he didn't know to what exactly Ted had resigned himself—the girls or his mopey little brother. Ted tipped his head back against the wall, switched the light off. It took a minute for Frank's eyes to adjust.

"Do these people mind us in their barn in the middle of the night?"

"The Epworths?" Ted said. "They're out of town. They have grand-kids in Kentucky or someplace."

He rooted around in his pockets, found what he was looking for, lit a match, and let it burn down between his fingers. He dropped the match, then twice repeated the procedure, each time letting the flame almost reach his fingertips before he shook it out.

"You know you met her once," he said.

"Mrs. Epworth?" Frank said.

"Heather Trout," Ted said. "You came up to visit me at school."

"The blonde? The one with the——"

"That was my date, Lilly something. Heather Trout was not the kind of girl you took to parties."

"I don't remember," Frank said.

Ted sat up and struck another match, his arms across his knees, his face halved by light and shadow.

"She had on this dress. It was awful but great, know what I mean? She didn't have any tits to speak of; she just had this look on her face all the time—I don't know—like lewd but in a good way."

"I don't remember," Frank said again.

"It doesn't matter," Ted said. He pushed his jaw from side to side with the heel of his free hand, tending to some tricky, personal chiropractic need. He said, "Tell me a story about a girl, Frank. Any love in your life? When's my little brother getting married?"

"There's nothing to tell."

Ted winced and sucked air over his teeth, and at first, Frank thought it was a reaction to what he'd said. Then Ted flipped the match away and cursed, as if he blamed it for burning him, and licked his thumb. The match had extinguished itself midflight, but it was still smoking so Frank walked over to where it landed and ground it out beneath his heel.

MARCY WAS DOZING on the couch when they got back, her ankles crossed, her hands folded neatly in her lap, a Navajo blanket covering her from knee to breast. Beside her, on the fireplace, was a half-finished glass of milk and a crumb-dappled plate. Ted loomed over her a second, then tickled the bottoms of her bare feet. Her eyes fluttered, and she balled her hands into fists and stretched her arms over her head.

"I had a funny dream," she said.

Ted said, "You didn't leave Santa any S'mores."

"There's more in the pantry," she said. Then, to Frank, "For future reference, for when you have children of your own, you should always leave a little milk in Santa's glass. It adds a touch of authenticity. I don't know why really, but it's true."

"What did you dream?" Frank said.

"Oh," she said. "It was silly."

"Tell me," Frank said.

"I'm getting S'mores," Ted said, marching off in the direction of the kitchen. "Anybody want S'mores?"

"No, thank you," Marcy said. She palmed her forehead, as if checking her temperature, then her cheeks, then the back of her neck. She squinted at Frank. "Do you really wanna know?" she said.

"I really do," he said.

She drew her legs up beside her on the couch and arranged the blanket in her lap. Her hair was mussed, but in a particularly charming way, Frank thought, as if the room—the fireplace, the Brazilian cherry molding—was really a movie set and a crew of hairdressers had spent hours styling Marcy's coiffure to strike the perfect balance between realistically disheveled and believably together.

"Well," she said, "I'm sure it's just that the ponies are on my mind, but I dreamed I was a trick rider in the rodeo—and I've been scared of horses all my life—but there I was doing handstands in the saddle and riding two at once like they were water skis."

"That's a laugh," Ted said, swinging back into the room, his voice a mumble because of the cookie in his mouth. "Marcy's terrified of horses."

"I just told him that," Marcy said.

"It's a good dream," Frank said.

"I had on this sequined leotard," Marcy said, sounding, Frank thought, rather wistful. "And a rhinestone belt with a big buckle. Can you stand it? I don't know what it means."

"I never remember my dreams," Frank said.

"You have to wake up in the middle," Marcy said.

Ted stood, chewing, behind the couch.

"Marcy used to keep a dream book. She took a class."

"I was just bored," she said. She blushed prettily and waved her hand beside her ear as if to consign the subject over her shoulder and into the past where it belonged. "It's time for bed," she said. She walked over and held Frank's hand and led him toward the stairs. "Let's get you settled. I'll show you where we keep the linens."

"I'll be right behind you," Ted said. "Just lemme get the lights."

On the landing, Marcy touched a finger to her lips and paused to listen at the twins' door. Satisfied, evidently, by the silence, she tiptoed past, and Frank followed her to his room, two doors down. She opened the closet and showed him a stack of quilts—in case he got cold, she said—and told him about the cabinet in the bathroom where they kept the extra towels. When she was finished, Marcy sat on the corner of the bed.

"We're glad you're here, Frank," she said. She crossed her legs and cupped her hand over her knee. "I know he doesn't like to make a big deal out of it, but family means the world to Ted. Ever since your mother died—" She paused, brushed a wayward strand of hair behind her ear. "Your father—" Another pause, a plaintive smile. "Well, you know how Ted feels about your father."

"You guys are great to have me," Frank said.

"We love you, Frank," she said. "If I didn't have Ted—" She shook her finger at him as if he'd made an inappropriate but not unappreciated remark. "If Ted weren't the sweetest thing—" Marcy pushed abruptly to her feet and kissed him on the cheek.

"I love you guys, too," he said.

"If you're interested," she said, "we could set an alarm to wake you up in the middle of your dream. That's what they made us do in class. We had to get up and write it down before we forgot. Everybody dreams. It's just a matter of remembering."

"I'll try anything," he said.

He heard Ted's footsteps on the stairs, then silence, then his voice in the twins' room, low and angry, then his footsteps in the hall. Ted burst into the guest room and said, "The little sneaks were *sleeping* together. You believe that? When I explicitly, *explicitly,* told them to stay in their own beds. You heard me, Frank. I made myself perfectly clear."

"It's Christmas, Ted," Marcy said. "Leave the girls alone."

Ted glared at his wife. "We've talked about the slippery slope," he said. He threw himself backward onto the mattress and linked his fingers under his neck. "I don't see what's so hard to understand."

"It's late," Marcy said. "Merry Christmas, Frank."

Without another word, she drifted out of the room and closed the door behind her. Frank stretched out beside his brother and pressed his eyes with the heels of his hands. Ted drew in a breath, as if to speak, then released it through his nose.

"What?" Frank said.

Ted said, "Nothing."

"What is it?" Frank said.

"I was just gonna mention that window," Ted said and right away Frank knew that Ted had changed the subject. "It was a picture window when we moved in, but it didn't suit the house so we put in divided-light."

For a minute, neither of them spoke. Frank listened to the steady rush of air in the heating ducts, the draw and sigh of his brother's heavy breathing. He pinched his nostrils closed with two fingers and, in a nasal voice, said, "I'm happy for you, Ted."

Ted propped up on his elbow and looked at Frank.

"What's that voice? Are you making fun of me?"

"No," Frank said.

Ted kept looking.

"I'm not," Frank said.

When Ted was gone, Frank got up and went into the bathroom to wash his face and brush his teeth. Back in the bedroom, he stripped to his boxers and hunched over his duffel bag for a minute, but he had forgotten what he wanted. He drew the covers back and climbed into bed. He knew, as soon as he closed his eyes, that he wouldn't be able to sleep, but he lay there hoping for half an hour. Finally, he gave up and headed for the kitchen to fix a glass of milk. Halfway to the stairs, he noticed an identical pair of heads, one over the other, peeking at him around a door frame.

"Hey girls," he said.

The twins said, "Uncle Frank?"

"It's me," he said. "You girls should be asleep."

They said, "We thought you might be Santa Claus."

"How do you do that? Do you always know what your sister's gonna say?"

"I guess," they said.

"It's like some kind of echo," he said. "It's like there's something fishy with my satellite feed."

The twins blinked. "Did Santa come?" they said.

"Not yet," he said.

"Do we have to go back to bed?"

"He won't come if you're awake."

They looked at each other, then back at Frank.

"Will you stay with us until we fall asleep?"

"All right," he said.

He followed the twins into their room, watched without comment as they climbed into the same bed, a four-poster with a muslin canopy. There was an identical bed not eight feet away, along with duplicate nightstands and chests of drawers and matching ice cream parlor chairs, everything done in shades of white, each side of the room a moonlit reflection of the other. "Do you think we'll get a pony for Christmas?" they said. Frank told them he wouldn't be surprised. He tucked the blanket in around them. He listened to them breathing in perfect rhythm in the dark. He stood there, like a sentry, until he was sure that they were dreaming.

At six o'clock the next morning, the twins dashed past the menagerie of gifts around the tree and out the back door to greet the ponies, who were tethered to a picnic table. Ted had brought them around while everyone was still asleep. Frank stood at the bay window in the living room and watched his brother lead them around the yard. The twins weren't so much riding as engaged in mounted hugs — each had her arms wrapped around a pony's neck, her cold face pressed into a mane. Marcy touched his elbow, and Frank started. She smiled sleepily and handed him a cup of coffee, then went outside with the video recorder and got everything on tape. Ted hammed it up for the camera. In his red flannel pajamas and his duck boots and his parka, he strutted like the leader of a marching band.

After a while, Marcy clapped her hands and hustled everyone back indoors. They opened presents. Frank had brought old-timey quilted dolls and costume jewelry for the twins. They weren't particularly impressed, but they thanked him at Marcy's prompting, and Marcy oohed and ahhed. He'd spent weeks looking for his gifts, but they embarrassed him now, struck him as quaint and inappropriate, when they had seemed perfect in the store.

Then — quite suddenly, it seemed to Frank — they were running late for church. The morning dissolved in a flurry of preparation. The girls had to be bathed, and Marcy had to do her hair, and somebody had to take the ponies back over to the barn. Frank volunteered. It only took him a few minutes to shower and get into his suit, and when he was dressed and ready, he led the ponies around the house and down the quiet street, their hooves clopping on the pavement. He'd never spent much time around horses, and he worried that something might happen on the way — a car would speed past and the ponies would rear up kicking like tiny broncos and bolt into the woods — but the trip was uneventful.

After church, Ted drove through town on the way to Marcy's parents' house—past a restaurant built into the old train depot and a drugstore with a soda fountain and an antique movie house. Everything was tinseled and garlanded and spangled with Christmas lights. Marcy's parents lived in a neighborhood thick with bungalows and oaks. They had moved up from D.C. the year before to be near the grandkids. Colonel Hammond (U.S. Air Force, retired) waved as they pulled into the drive and propped the front door open with his hip. The twins burst out of the car and rushed the house and buried their faces in Colonel Hammond's lap before ducking past him through the door. Colonel Hammond welcomed Frank with a slap on the back and ushered them all inside, Marcy, then Frank, then Ted, carrying a laundry basket full of gifts. In the living room, Frank was introduced to Mr. and Mrs. Lattimore, the Hammonds' neighbors and steadfast bridge partners, and he kissed Mrs. Hammond, who was kneeling beside the Christmas tree with the twins, pointing out particular presents and urging them to guess the contents. Frank had the disorienting sense that time was proceeding at an accelerated pace. Colonel Hammond was pressing a hot toddy into his hand, and Mr. Lattimore was saying how fond they had become of Ted and Marcy and the girls, and Mrs. Lattimore was asking how Frank had liked Ted and Marcy's church.

"You know it's where they bless the hounds," she said.

"The what?"

"The hounds," Marcy said. "For hunting foxes."

"Ah," Frank said.

"It's quite a spectacle," Mrs. Lattimore said. "The bishop comes down from Baltimore and the hounds are baying and all the hunters are in red and black. They've been at it for a hundred years."

Mrs. Hammond said, "I'm just sorry your father couldn't come. We haven't seen your father since the wedding."

"Wouldn't come," Ted corrected.

"I don't get that," Colonel Hammond said. He narrowed his eyes and aimed his finger at Ted's comment as if it was still hanging in the air.

Mrs. Hammond said, "Ron, you don't know."

"He's had a hard time," Frank said. "He likes to be alone."

"He's an asshole," Ted said.

Marcy said, "Ted," and tipped her head in the direction of the twins.

"I can't see missing Christmas with these girls to save the world," Colonel Hammond said.

They paused a moment to marvel at the twins, who were passing packages back and forth, listening intently to the sounds the boxes made, then Mrs. Lattimore picked up the thread of conversation.

"If I might," she said. "From the perspective of a childless couple—" She hesitated, gathered her thoughts. "Well, I agree with Colonel Ron. I just don't understand how your father could choose to spend the holidays away from his family. You have no *idea* what Oscar and I—" Here she broke off, and Mr. Lattimore put his hand gently on her shoulder.

"Hey now," he said. "Easy now."

Frank said, "Would somebody point me in the direction of the restroom?"

He pushed to his feet and raised his eyebrows. Colonel Hammond told him the latrine was down the hallway on the left. Frank locked the door. Behind him was a second entrance, and he locked that door as well, then sat on the lid of the toilet and dropped his face into his hands. His palms were clammy and cold. He stayed like that, breathing through his fingers, until he heard singing and piano music down the hall.

THEY WERE POLISHING off "Jingle Bells" when he found them at the baby grand. Mr. Lattimore was playing the piano, souping things up with ragtime flourishes. Marcy was sitting beside him on the bench with a twin on either leg, and Ted was behind her, hands on his hips, looking game but anxious, and Colonel Hammond was next to Ted. He waved Frank over as Mr. Lattimore swung into "Frosty the Snowman." Mrs. Lattimore had pulled a chair up on her husband's left. Frank guessed that Mrs. Hammond had adjourned to the kitchen to put the finishing touches on the meal. He took a position beside his brother, sang when he knew the words. They did "Santa Claus Is Coming to Town" and "Deck the Halls," then a "Jingle Bells" reprise at the twins' request. Finally, Mrs. Hammond called them in for dinner. As if from a great distance, Frank heard himself gushing over Mrs. Hammond's spread — breast of quail in mushroom gravy, served with wild rice and braised asparagus — heard himself making shop talk with Mr. Lattimore, who had earned his nut writing jingles for radio and television ads.

"You remember Oxydol?"

"The detergent?" Frank said.

Mr. Lattimore smirked and bobbed his head.

"That was me," he said. "I did that one."

"No kidding," Frank said.

"You know they're bringing Oxydol back," Mrs. Lattimore said, stroking her husband's bicep. "We're hoping they'll use Oscar's jingle on TV."

"We've got our fingers crossed," Mr. Lattimore said.

He crossed his fingers on both hands.

From the far end of the table, Ted said, "Given enough time everything makes a comeback," and Frank wondered if his brother wasn't on the verge of being drunk.

When the meal was finished, they separated into groups: women to the breakfast table in the kitchen, men to Colonel Hammond's study. There was a manual typewriter on the desk and a couch and a battered leather chair and a hassock upholstered in horsehide. Colonel Hammond fixed them each a Grand Marnier, and they did a quick roundtable on current events, the recent election mess, all the counting and recounting and the new president's chances. Colonel

Hammond and Mr. Lattimore deferred to Ted on the political fine points. Ted made cryptic references to acquaintances on the hill. Frank was about to offer his opinion on the tax cut, when Colonel Hammond looked at him and said, "How old are you exactly?"

After a moment, Frank said, "I turned thirty in October."

He glared at Ted, as if for confirmation. Ted nodded and grinned and sipped his drink.

"You're a decent-looking kid," Colonel Hammond said. "You must know a lot of women." He paused, closed both hands around his glass, set the glass before him on the desk.

"Not as many as you'd think," Frank said.

The room was quiet for a moment. Frank heard a burst of laughter from the kitchen. At some point, his drink had lapped over the lip of his glass and now his fingers felt adhesive.

Mr. Lattimore said, "I knew this woman once—this was pre-Vivian, this was in New York when I was doing jazz—I knew this girl who was always hanging round the clubs." He snapped his fingers and shimmied in his chair. "This girl had a thing for musicians. This girl would perform carnal acts that are illegal in forty-seven states."

"I was stationed in the Philippines," Colonel Hammond said. "Don't tell me about carnal acts."

Frank glanced at Ted, waited for his brother to say something about Heather Trout, but Ted was gazing out the window and kept his own counsel on the matter, and Frank liked him for it. Then he decided that Ted was just being a proper son-in-law, avoiding the discussion for Colonel Hammond's sake. He watched Ted tug his shirt cuff over the heel of his hand and swipe at a blemish on the glass. There was another roll of laughter from the kitchen. Frank pushed to his feet, excused himself, entered the bathroom from the study, and left it through the door into the hall. The twins were in the living room, playing with a collection of porcelain figurines, cooking up elaborate romances—the ballerina loved the unicorn, the unicorn loved the cat, the cat loved the clown. The kitchen door was open so Marcy could keep an eye on things. He could see her at the table, smiling over the rim of a coffee mug, her hair drawn into a ponytail, her exposed neck slender and elegant and gilded with fugitive, light-catching wisps. Frank could hear pieces of all three conversations. In the kitchen, Mrs. Lattimore said, "It's such a shame." In the study, Colonel Hammond said, "I'm telling you, she had apparatus." And in the living room, one of the twins said, "Bozo doesn't love Miss Kitty anymore." He closed his eyes, listened for her sister's reply. "It's such a shame," she said. He couldn't make out a difference in their voices.

"YOU REALLY DON'T remember Heather Trout?" Ted said. They were at the picnic table, drinking Ted's good scotch and watching Marcy lead the twins on a pony ride around the yard. This was half past five, the party long over, the day's last light clinging to the sky. The girls were maybe a hundred yards away. Ted poked his finger in his glass and fished a piece of flotsam out.

"I really don't," Frank said.

"How could you forget?" Ted said, disappointed. "Brown hair and eyes. She had this little gap between her teeth." He pointed at his mouth. "I'm telling you, Heather Trout was wild. That time you came up to visit, I gave it to her in the john. She's up on the sink, and I've got my pants around my ankles, and my date is knocking on the door." He shook his head. "Marcy thinks wild is when we leave the light on."

They were quiet for a minute. Frank didn't know what Ted wanted him to say. He watched Marcy lead the girls back toward the patio, her hair pressed around her face by a stocking cap.

"Take a pony from me," she said. "They want to go double for a while."

Ted gave Frank a knowing look.

"I don't think that's such a hot idea," he said. "I don't think we want to set a precedent."

"Don't be ridiculous," Marcy said.

She smiled brightly at her husband, handed Frank a lead. She lifted one twin off her pony and put her in the saddle behind the other. "Hold on to your sister," she said. She leaned against the rope, but the pony didn't budge. She made a clicking sound with her tongue. The pony huffed. Marcy stiffened, breathed deep, brushed the hair out of her face. Without looking at him, she muttered, "Ted, help." Ted did a meaningful grunt. He stood, slapped the pony lightly on the rump. The pony skittered forward a few steps, then planted its hooves, an imitation of a sawhorse, and the startled twins began to cry. There was a moment, just before their bawling became audible, when the twins were poised in time—wide-eyed and open-mouthed, as if they had just experienced a terrible epiphany. Then the air was split with sobs, and Ted and Marcy each snatched a twin out of the saddle and whisked them inside, leaving Frank alone with the offending pony and his compatriot.

The ponies, however, were unperturbed. They gazed at the river for a moment, as if something that Frank couldn't see was arresting their attention, then flared their nostrils and, simultaneously, exhaled in what he could only have described as a world-weary sigh. He had assumed that they were young—because of their size, he thought. Now, he wondered if Ted had procured a pair of old birthday party veterans or petting zoo retirees.

"How old are you?" he said.

One of them, the stubborn one, looked around at Frank in such a way that he worried it was about to reply, but it dropped its head without speaking and picked at the grass that pushed up through the snow.

Frank said, "What's your problem?"

The pony didn't answer.

"What's the matter with you?" he said.

The pony kept him in the dark.

Frank heard a flare of voices from inside. A minute later, Ted appeared on the patio and announced that Marcy wanted them to return the ponies to the barn and feed Mrs. Epworth's cat. They made the trip in silence. Night had settled in. When the ponies had been safely stowed, their gear all put away, Ted let them into the house with a key tied to a blue ribbon. He ignored the cat (a fat, white Persian) and passed through the kitchen and the dining room and into a room that, in another time, would have been referred to as a parlor. It was decorated in prim, fragile-looking antiques. Frank was put in mind of Marie Antoinette. His brother hit the lights, did a long, appraising survey, the cat weaving figure eights between his ankles.

"I hate this house," he said.

He nudged the cat with his foot. The cat paced into the kitchen, circled back, rubbed its muzzle on Ted's shoe.

"It's like nobody *lives* here," he said. "It makes me tired."

"I guess," Frank said.

"Three months and fifty thousand bucks, I'd whip this sucker into shape. Dump all this furniture and strip the wallpaper and take down the wall into the dining room."

"I think it's sort of nice," Frank said.

"I'm not talking about nice," Ted said. "I'm talking about creating space."

The cat slipped between his legs and once more padded toward the kitchen. Ted followed it this time. Frank waited while he spooned soft food into a bowl and filled a water dish. Ted washed his hands and cut the lights, and they headed home again. Moonlight had turned the trees into ragged silhouettes. A handful of stars glimmered behind the canopy of branches.

"You remember that wig Mom had?" Frank said. "Blond and short. The last one she bought, I think."

Ted stopped in the middle of the road.

"What about it?" he said.

"I don't know," Frank said. "Nothing, I guess. I was just thinking how much Dad liked that wig." He walked backwards a few steps.

"Here we go," Ted said.

They faced each other, not more than a dozen yards apart.

"It's Christmas," Frank said. "We should call him."

Ted said, "You call him if you want. As far as I'm concerned, he can call me if he has something he wants to say."

"I don't think he likes us very much," Frank said.

"He doesn't *like* us?" Ted said. "What's *wrong* with you?"

"He thinks it was too easy for us, you know. He thinks we didn't mourn her long enough. He thinks we just went back to our lives."

"It's been five years," Ted said. "I tell you what—if you talk to him, you tell him I don't like him back."

With that, Ted started walking again, his arms swinging, his feet scuffing the pavement. Frank watched his brother stride from shadow to pool of moonlight, back again to shadow. Then he heard a sound in the woods (footstep? fallen limb?) and he hurried to catch up.

THEY HAD HAM sandwiches for dinner. Marcy made a salad with toasted walnuts and bleu cheese to go with the leftovers, and they carried their plates into the family room to watch a bowl game on TV. The twins had eaten while Ted and Frank were down the street. They were sprawled on the carpet now with a variety of dolls.

"Colleen, baby, back up a little," Ted said. "Daddy can't see TV."

Neither twin responded. Marcy had dressed them in matching yellow pajamas. One of them had a group of dolls sitting in a row like they were on a bus. The other arranged a male doll's arms over his head, balanced him on the lip of the television and guided him on a long, elegant cliff dive. Ted stood, lifted that one by her armpits and carried her three feet from the TV. Then he returned to his chair and brought his sandwich to his lips, leaving a smear of mustard at the corner of his mouth.

"How do you tell them apart?" Frank said.

Ted kept his eyes on the TV.

Marcy said, "It's not so hard. Colleen is a little taller. Jane Margaret has a beauty mark on her shoulder. It was harder when they were babies. Don't you remember? We had to paint Jane Margaret's fingernails. Her fingernails were small as lemon seeds."

"Hear that, girls?" Ted said. "Uncle Frank can't tell you apart." He dropped his sandwich on his plate and walked over and stood between the twins. "I'd like to conduct a little experiment," he said, loudly. "On your feet." The twins put down their dolls.

Marcy said, "What're you doing?"

"This'll be fun," Ted said. "Frank, close your eyes."

"I don't think I want to do this," Frank said.

Ted stared until Frank did as he instructed. Frank could hear Ted whispering. The twins giggled. A few seconds later, Ted told him it was all right to look, and he opened his eyes to find the twins stationed on either side of their father. Ted had a hand on each blond head.

"Who's who?" he said.

Frank studied the twins, tried to recognize some dissimilarity in their faces. He couldn't see a difference. Round cheeks, full lips, dainty ears—all identical. He noticed matching blue crescents under their eyes, and he wondered if the blemishes were the result of ordinary Santa Claus anticipation or some more pressing and personal girlish worry.

"I have to make a phone call," he said.

Ted said, "Answer the question first."

Marcy glanced from Frank to Ted and back to Frank.

"What is all this?" she said.

Frank stood and collected his napkin and his plate and stalked out of the room. Behind him, Marcy said, "Let *me* guess then. You must be Colleen?" The twins laughed and laughed at her pretend mistake. Frank left his plate in the kitchen sink, trotted up the stairs to his room, stretched out on the bed, took a moment to collect himself. There was a phone on the nightstand, and Frank rolled onto his side and lifted the handset. He listened to the dial tone for a moment, then hung up and swung his legs over the side of the bed. He picked up the phone again and cradled the receiver in his lap. This time he dialed his father's number. He could hear it ringing—remote, inconsequential. Then he heard a distant voice and brought the receiver to his ear.

"Dad?" he said.

"Ted?"

"It's me," he said. "It's Frank."

"I thought you were your brother."

"I figured," Frank said.

There was rustling on the line and he imagined his father getting organized in his easy chair, patting his breast pocket for his glasses.

"What time is it?" his father said.

"I don't know," Frank said. "Maybe nine o'clock."

"I fell asleep," his father said. "I was watching this football game on TV and I fell asleep." He laughed softly. "I'm an old man," he said.

"Did you have a nice Christmas?" Frank said.

"I spent a few hours with your mother. They really let the cemetery go this time of year. Just because it's December doesn't mean they shouldn't provide an attractive resting place."

"Did you open your presents?" Frank said.

"Not yet," his father said.

"You should open your presents, Dad."

"I know," his father said. "I will."

They were quiet for a second.

His father said, "How are the twins?"

"They're great," Frank said. "They're beautiful."

"Ted should bring them down to see your mother. Those girls have never been to see your mother's grave."

"They got ponies for Christmas," Frank said.

"Ponies?" his father said. "Lord."

"You should open your presents," Frank said. "There might be a pony in one of those packages for you."

"I'm too old for ponies. Can you return a pony to the store? Can you take a pony back if it isn't what you wanted?"

"I doubt it," Frank said.

Just then, there was gentle rapping at the door and Frank asked his father to hold on. He covered the mouthpiece with his hand. "Who is it?" he said, and Marcy opened the door and poked her head into the room. "I'm sorry to interrupt," she said. "The girls are off to bed. They want to say goodnight." She pressed her lips together. "When you're finished," she said. "Just take your time." Then Marcy closed the door, and Frank listened to her footsteps receding down the hall.

"Is that Ted?" his father said. "Does he want to talk?"

"It was Marcy," Frank said. "She's putting the girls to bed."

"Ah," his father said.

"Ted told me to tell you merry Christmas though. He said to tell you merry Christmas and he loves you."

"Tell him I said it back," his father said.

"I'll do that."

"Well," his father said.

"Right," Frank said.

"I have presents to open."

"Right," Frank said. "Merry Christmas, Dad."

His father said, "Hey, buddy, Christmas is just getting started over here. I might already have a new pony in the house. You said so yourself. Your mother would get a kick out of a pony." With that, he disconnected, leaving perfect silence where his voice had been. Frank stayed where he was, listening to nothing on the line, until the phone began to make a buzzing sound, and he hung up. There was a rushing in his head like he was listening to a seashell. After a minute, he made his way down the hall to the twins' room. Marcy had just finished tucking them in. She put a hand on Frank's arm and steered him in between the beds and gave him a look, half pleading, half amused. "Now, listen, girls," she said. "Uncle Frank knows. He'll tell you it's better if you sleep in separate beds."

The twins each had an arm on top of the blankets, an arm beneath — one right, one left, a flawless mirror image.

"Your mother's right," Frank said.

"Why?" they said.

He looked at Marcy. Marcy shrugged.

"Where's Ted?" he said.

"He's been in already," Marcy said. "You know Ted's style. He delivers his ultimatum and expects to be obeyed." She slipped her arm in the crook of his elbow, bumped him with her hip. "I'll leave you guys alone," she said. Before Frank could protest, she winked and blew the girls a kiss and skipped into the hall, closing the door behind her.

The twins said, "Why can't we sleep together?"

"There must be a good reason," he said. "I just can't think of it right now." He paused. "Why do you want to sleep together?"

"I don't know," they said.

He leaned against a bedpost and crossed his arms.

"I'm sorry about before," he said.

"Why?" they said.

"I couldn't tell you two apart."

"I'm Jane," one said, and the other said, "I'm Colleen." Each glanced slyly at her sister. They were only able to maintain their deception for an instant before they collapsed into hysterics and kicked their feet under the covers. Frank laughed out loud.

"You think that's pretty funny?" he said.

"Yes," they said.

"I do too," he said.

Two hours later, Frank woke panting and desperate and not at all sure where he was. The room smelled vaguely of paint. Shadows assumed unfamiliar shapes against the walls. He blinked and rubbed his eyes and one of the shadows moved, giving him a start. Then a stripe of moonlight fell across it and he recognized Marcy standing at the foot of the bed.

"I didn't mean to scare you," she said.

"What is it?" he said. "Is something wrong?"

"No, no," she said. "I just forgot to wake you up last night. You know, about remembering your dream. I couldn't sleep. I thought I'd see if maybe you're still interested."

"Oh," he said.

Marcy was wearing a terry cloth headband and a nightshirt and wool socks. The shirt said #1 MOM in rainbow letters across the front. The moonlight made her legs look bright as ice.

"I'm sorry," she said. "I shouldn't have."

"It's all right," he said.

"Do you remember anything?"

"Let's see," he said. He pushed himself upright, propped his back against the headboard, reached for the lamp, but Marcy said, "Leave it off. The dark helps sometimes."

Frank closed his eyes and searched his memory for a residue of his dream. He felt the mattress shift with Marcy's weight. He opened his eyes and saw her perched on the corner of the bed.

"Nothing?" she said.

"I remember trees," he lied, not wanting to disappoint her. "I remember birds."

"That's a start," she said. She crossed her legs and pinched her lower lip between two fingers. The next thing she said caught Frank off guard. She laid back on the bed and rolled onto her stomach and bent her knees so that her legs were swinging in the air behind her.

"What do you think of Ted?" she said.

"I don't think anything," Frank said after a moment. "He's my brother."

"I know you have your differences," Marcy said, "and Ted will probably never forgive your father for not coming up here when the girls were born, and I'm sure you think that he's too strict."

"Ted's right," Frank said. "Dad should've come."

Marcy looked at him a second.

"Would you mind if I put my head on your shoulder?"

Frank swallowed and shook his head. Marcy crawled toward him, rested her cheek on his chest. She drew his arm over her like a shawl. A strand of her hair was tickling his nose. "Do you have someone, Frank?" she said. "It makes me sad to think of you alone."

"I have someone," he said.

"Do you really? Who? Tell me, what's her name?"

He blew the hair out of his face.

"Heather Trout," he said.

"That's a funny name."

"Heather's a funny girl," he said.

"Tell me about her."

"I'll tell you this much—Heather shaves her pubic hair."

Marcy gasped and slapped his stomach.

"No?" she said. *"Really?"*

"It's true," he said.

In a small voice, she said, "Do you like it?"

"I don't mind," he said.

"You're terrible," she said.

Marcy adjusted her head on his chest. He could feel her breath sifting through his T-shirt. His skin was warm and electric where they touched. "Don't let me fall asleep," she said, and he told her that he wouldn't, but it wasn't long before he sensed her breathing slow, her muscles softening against him. He didn't know how she could sleep with his heart pounding beneath her ear. He let her rest until his arm began to tingle. Then he shook her gently awake and Marcy sat up in bed and combed her fingers through her hair. "Oh," she said, her voice filled with wonder, "I dreamed I was in a caravan in the desert. Except instead of camels we had ponies. They had chests of rare spices and jewels and magic carpets on their backs."

"You're making that up," he said.

"I'm not," she said. "I swear."

"I wish I had dreams like that," he said.

Marcy touched his chin with her index finger. "You do," she said. "You've let them slip your mind is all." Then she stood and flipped her hair over her shoulder and left him in the dark.

FRANK OVERSLEPT IN the morning. He could have gone on dozing forever, but it was after ten o'clock by the time he dragged himself awake, and he didn't want his brother to think he made a habit of sleeping late. He stepped into his pants from the night before and pulled his undershirt over his head and bumbled downstairs, hoping Ted and Marcy had left a little coffee in the pot. As he approached the kitchen, he heard Marcy's voice — high-pitched, intent — and he stopped shy of the door and listened.

"They're afraid," she said.

"And coddling them isn't going to help," Ted said. "In the long run, coddling never did anybody any good."

"Just wait a day or two. It's my fault they're scared. I don't want to rush them into anything. I don't want to make it worse, Ted. In a couple of days, they'll have forgotten about being scared."

"There's an old saying about this, Marcy."

"I know, but—"

"It applies," Ted said.

"Yes, but—"

"There has never been a more perfect application."

"Fine," Marcy said.

Frank backpedaled a few steps, then turned and tiptoed down the hall. He heard the television muttering in the family room and followed the sound. The twins were watching the Christmas morning video on the VCR. They were lying on their bellies on the carpet, chins resting on identically folded arms. On screen, Ted goaded the ponies into a gentle trot, and the twins shrieked with laughter. Frank sat on the couch. He told them good morning and they replied in kind without looking at him.

"You girls riding today?" he said.

"Dad's making us," they said.

"Have you named the ponies yet?"

The twins glanced at him over their shoulders.

"No," they said.

"Any ideas?" he said.

"No," they said.

"You know your father and I are named after famous presidents."

They didn't answer.

"Teddy and Franklin Roosevelt," he said. "Do you have a teddy bear?"

The twins sat up and looked at him.

"Yes," they said.

"Teddy bears are named after Teddy Roosevelt," he said.

Marcy arrived, still wearing her nightshirt. She said, "Hello, Frank," and gave him a shy, embarrassed smile and hustled the twins off to bathe. Frank headed for the kitchen and found Ted sitting on the counter, his eyes fixed on the microwave. The room smelled buttery and warm.

"How long have you been up?" Ted said.

"Not too long—I've been talking to the twins." He pointed at the coffee pot. There were a few inches of coffee in the bottom.

Ted said, "Help yourself."

"Mugs?"

"In the cabinet," Ted said.

Frank found a cup and filled it and leaned against the stove facing his brother.

Ted said, "I think there are still some muffins in the oven."

"I'm not hungry," Frank said.

"You should eat," Ted said, but Frank could tell his heart wasn't in it. Ted hopped down from the counter and moved the breakfast dishes from the sink into the dishwasher. He poured detergent and flipped the switch. A pass-through looked out from there into the dining room, and Ted crossed his arms and gazed in that direction.

"What were you and the girls talking about?"

"They haven't named the ponies," Frank said. "We talked about that."

"That's good," Ted said.

"I told them Dad named us after the Roosevelts."

Ted turned his head just enough so that Frank could see the angle of his chin. He seemed about to object, then thought better of it and sighed and bridged a hand over his eyes.

"There used to be a wall here," he said. "The pass-through opens things up. Don't you think? And now you can hand food into the dining room without having to carry plates all the way around."

"It looks great," Frank said.

After a moment, Ted snapped his hand away from his brow like a salute and marched out of the kitchen. Frank swiped a muffin from the oven, carried it back to his room. He stood at the window, listening to the murmur of girlish voices down the hall. Beyond the windows, across the lawn, the river moved imperceptibly toward he knew not where. It had to go someplace, he thought. He must have known its destination sometime, but he couldn't remember now. He tossed the uneaten muffin in the trash, then felt guilty and wasteful and picked it out and wiped it clean and forced himself to eat.

Christmas Holidays

by Ellen Douglas

S is and Alderan had already been divorced in the winter of 1935 when Anna spent part of her Christmas holidays with her grandmother. Sis was at home again in the evenings after supper when the family gathered in the dining room for the day's "visiting"; Sis, and Gran, and Sarah D., and Charlie Dupré, who was working in Homochitto that winter, and little Charlotte, and the baby, four-year-old Billy.

The dining room was unchanged by the five years that had passed since Sis's marriage, except that it was dingier, the floors more splintery, the upholstery stained and worn in a few new places. The Empire day bed still stood against the wall below the huge mirror that still seemed about to fall and crush whoever happened to be lying under it; the big platform rocker still sat by the fireplace where anyone who passed might bruise his shin on it; the mayonnaise stain still marked the floor by the parlor door. The one change that had taken place in the house was that it no longer belonged to Kate. Unable to keep up the mortgage payments, the family had lost the house to the Building and Loan Company and now rented it. Sis had lost Alderan, the family had lost the house, and Anna, too, had suffered a loss. Marjorie was gone. She did not look for her in the mirror because she had a new love. Sometime during the winter of her eleventh year she had begun to read with the voracious absorption of childhood and Marjorie had gone away, replaced by Mowgli, Tarzan, Bomba the Jungle Boy, Jo March, Elsie Dinsmore, and the Little Colonel. The first winter she had been struck by this new passion, she had read the *Book of Knowledge*, all twenty-four volumes, straight through, unselectively, and she had been so obsessed that if she was in the bathroom she would read all the fine print on the Lysol and milk of magnesia bottles. She wanted only books for Christmas, and the year she had gotten ten she remembered as the most satisfactory Christmas of her childhood. She was too shy to look for what she wanted in strange places, and so she did not discover the public library until she was in high school. In her grandmothers' houses she was limited to the curious collections in their tall glass-fronted bookcases. The McGoverns, of course, had an overweening passion for theology and religious history; even Anna's obsession was balked by the multivolume *History of the Reformation*, Foxe's *Book of Martyrs*, the collections of sermons, and the *Decline and Fall of the Roman Empire*. When she was thirteen, she read straight through the four volumes of *The Rise of the Dutch Republic*, but that was a dull summer. At Kate Anderson's house she had to choose among an illassorted collection of remnants. Will was a reader, and he had taken the sets of Dickens, Thackeray, Scott, and Cooper to New Orleans. All that were left were a few of the great-grandfather's medical books, a set of Presbyterian moral stories for children called *Line upon Line, Precept upon Precept,* the Rollo books for boys, and some odds and ends, mostly popular novels, acquired during a brief period of prosperity in the 1890s.

This particular night, although she was scornfully conscious that she was too old for it, she was lying on the day bed, reading *Rollo at Eton.* Sis had gone to a movie with Caroline Bell; Sarah D., sitting by the fire in the platform rocker, was reading *The Delineator,* Charlie and Gran had drawn two straight-backed chairs up to the dining room table and were cracking and picking out pecans.

But Anna did not read as absorbedly as usual. Something was going on in her family, something that made her restless and excited, something fascinating and tragic that she did not understand. She could not have kept her attention even on the climactic scene of *Elsie Dinsmore,* the moment when Elsie faints at the piano because her father has forced her to play profane music on Sunday. As for Rollo, she had always had a feeling that he was a sissy, although the author did not seem to know it, and now she read of his difficulties with his wicked cousin Basil abstractedly, chiefly out of the habit of having a book in her hand. In another part of her mind she examined snatches of conversation and tried to understand what her family's trouble was.

It's like the Lysol bottle, she thought to herself. *There's something about the label on the Lysol bottle that I don't understand. Now what is it?*

"Feminine hygiene," the advertisements said, and there was the worried lady in the picture, holding the Lysol bottle and frowning unhappily. What was she worried about? And how would Lysol solve her problems?

Mama thinks she's told me all about it, Anna said to herself, *and I understand what she said about babies and menstruating and all that, but where does the Lysol come in?*

"I don't know what to do about her," Gran was saying. "I'm at my wits' end. Do you know how much she weighs now, Charlie? *Seventy-eight pounds!* I don't see how she stays alive."

Sarah D. looked up from her magazine. "What worries me more than that is she's quit going to church," she said. "Now if it were *me,* that would be one thing. But for Sis not to go to church! That scares me."

Charlie bent over the nutcracker that was screwed to the edge of the dining room table, swung the handle rhythmically back and forth, and dropped the cracked nuts into a bowl in his lap. His words were punctuated by the creak of iron and the explosions of pecan shells.

"Now, let me tell you something, Mrs. A.," he said, "and you, too, Sarah D. I've had a lot more experience of the world than you all have and I've seen this kind of thing happen before. Why, I could have told you after ten minutes' conversation with Alderan how this thing would turn out." He laughed a rueful women-are-like-that laugh and put a pecan in his mouth. "Sis has had *me* over a barrel a couple of times," he said. "I know her. She ain't an easy woman to live with."

Kate shook her head impatiently. "Damn him," she said. "God damn him."

Shocked, Anna looked at her grandmother sadly. That was the sort of thing Elsie Dinsmore would have to pray over for weeks. But then, hearing the slow sound of the words ringing in her ears, she realized that her grandmother was not cursing thoughtlessly. It even sounded as if she might be praying. At any rate, she meant it. She meant God damn him. *So he must be awful,* Anna said to herself. *Even if I never thought so.*

"Now, Mrs. A.," Charlie said again, "let me tell you something. In the first place, she'll get over him. She'll pull out of it. Mark my words. She thinks she's never going to be the same again, but she will. She may even think she's going crazy, or that she's going to kill herself (goodness knows, you're right — she acts half crazy), but she won't. All you've got to do is be patient and give her time to settle down. She'll start going to church — in fact, I'll betcha she'll be going to prayer meeting within six months."

Sarah D. had gone back to her magazine and Charlie lowered his voice and nodded at Anna who sat cross-legged on the day bed, bent over her book. "Anna's the best medicine Sis could have right now," he said to Kate in a low voice. "She makes a big effort to be cheerful for her."

"Sometimes I almost hate her for making herself suffer so," Kate said half to herself. She pressed her lips and teeth together as if biting off an invisible thread and ran her hand through the wispy gray hair that was twisted into a knot on top of her head. Then she sighed. "I remember when she was a little thing, how she used to shut herself up in the closet to pray after she'd been punished. I feel now just like I did then. I want to rip open the door and shake some sense into her."

Charlie was pursuing his own thoughts. "I know one thing about it," he said. "If Sis had a little passion in her nature, it probably never would have happened." He shrugged in a half-embarrassed, half-superior way. "After all," he said, "a man wants a *woman* when he marries. Why do you think Alderan took up with this little gal in Maraisville? Sis just ain't made for marriage and she'll be better off without him—without any man, for that matter."

Kate looked at her tall, balding, paunchy son-in-law, and Anna watched her watching him. Then she looked at her uncle to see what it was Kate was looking at so fiercely. He was bent over the nutcracker, a half smile of tolerant understanding on his face. His small chin disappeared into the roll of fat around his jowls, and the long strands of black hair that he usually brushed carefully over his bald spot had fallen down on his high, shiny forehead. He put another pecan in his mouth, and his face, still handsome in repose, seemed to vanish into layers of moving fat, as he chewed it thoughtfully.

Anna knew that something had happened. She moved restlessly to a new position on the day bed, hanging her legs over the side and leaning back against the cushions at the head. She wished that Charlie would not talk so much and hoped that Kate would talk about something else. Although she wanted very much to hear everything they had to say about Sis and Alderan, she had the constricted feeling in her chest that came when grown people were angry with each other.

Kate continued to look at Charlie as if she had just remembered something unpleasant that she had failed to take into account. She watched him cracking nuts and her face was controlled and contemptuous.

At last she said, "You're eating all you pick out."

Charlie continued his exposition. "So you see," he said, "Alderan wasn't all to blame. You have to think about his side of it."

"*His* side of it!" Kate said. "I don't *care* about his side of it."

Charlie looked up at her. Then, "Oh, I'm not saying he wasn't at fault," he said. "Alderan's a little bit stupid, or he would have known Sis—known you *all* for . . ." He broke off. "Alderan's a good fellow," he said. "He's a good man to take on a hunting trip or—or a stag party. But he never had a clue about you—about *us*. About our kind of people. Especially the women."

Kate got up and got the whiskey bottle and the sugar bowl from the sideboard and brought them to the table. She put them down with a thump. "We ought not to talk about it," she said. "I get too mad. When I think . . . When I think what he did to Ralph and Charlotte, and then you say, *his side of it* . . ."

"As for Ralph," Charlie said, "Ralph has always been as naïve and trusting as a preacher. If he'd had his mind on his business, he'd have kept his warehouse locked up."

Kate silently sprinkled sugar on a few pecans in a glass and poured in some whiskey. She shook her head warningly at Charlie. "Do you want me to fix you some whiskey and pecans?" she asked.

But Anna had heard. "What are you talking about, Charlie?" she said.

"She's old enough to know," Charlie said. "It can't hurt her."

"You already know, darling, don't you?" Kate said. "You know that Alderan stole some money from your father last year and he had to fire him. And you know Sis and Alderan just got a divorce and Sis is living here now. You know all that."

"Oh," Anna said. "That. Give me some pecans and whiskey, Gran."

But I never did understand it all, she said to herself. *I never did know why he did it, when he was working for Father and everything. When Father gave him the job when he was broke. And he and Sis were living right there in the house with us and we were having such a good time. And he was right in the middle of teaching Katherine to drive. If it hadn't all happened he would have taught me to drive this year.*

A picture flashed into her mind, as vivid as that old picture of her grandmother saying in the parlor just before Sis and Alderan were married, "I could never marry a man who called a Chevrolet a Shivvy." Was it so important what you called a Chevrolet? A yawning abyss opened at the edge of her mind and she gazed into it, shivering and unhappy. Alderan stood on the bank of Lake Jackson with his hands on his hips looking at her and laughing. They had been fishing all day, she and Alderan and Sis and Katherine; he had just dragged the boat up on the bank ready to go home.

Sometime in the course of the day they had decided to go through a narrow channel between the upper and the lower parts of the lake, a little twisting canal choked with brush and rotting logs and jutting cypress knees. Halfway through, the boat had stuck on a mud bank and Alderan had climbed happily out, knee-deep in mud, to shove it through. Sis had sat rigid in the boat, muttering admonitions from time to time about water moccasins, while the children giggled with excitement.

"Hey, girls, the water's fine. Won't you join me?" he had said, as he strained and pushed and sweated and rocked the boat, stirring up whirlpools of mud-black water.

Sis had said over and over, "Look out for holes, darling. For God's sake, don't step in a hole," for Alderan couldn't swim and wouldn't wear a life preserver.

"We'll save him," Anna and Katherine had shouted joyfully. "We'll save him if he steps in a hole."

The boat had rocked and swung and scraped across the mud, and finally slipped into deeper water, and Alderan had climbed back in, his old, oil-stained khaki pants and ragged tennis shoes clotted and rank with slimy black mud, his shirt torn across the shoulders by a thorn branch; and they had gone on fishing.

Now, in her mind, Alderan stood on the bank and looked at her. The black mud had dried to a crust on his pants and shoes, and a long smear had dried across his cheek and forehead. His shirt was dark with sweat stains across his back and under his arms, and he smelled like sweat and fish. He was smiling at her, the low, western sun striking into his eyes and making him screw up his good-natured, leathery face. She must have said something to him and he had said in reply, "I'll bet you never saw your *father* look like this in your whole life." At twelve she had laughed, and he had laughed and that was the end of the scene; but at fourteen the surface of her memory of it was pierced by doubt, by the beginning of a painful understanding, and she felt her heart contract in embarrassment.

For already there was beginning to work in Anna the combination of qualities that were always to torment and support her. She had a sure sense of the reality of the action that went on around her and an unfaltering memory for its climactic moments. The fabric of events, the content of scene after scene in her life, stuck persistently in her mind whether or not she could assimilate it and understand it. Far from forgetting or transforming the painful moments that children are generally supposed to suppress, she could *never* forget them, and year by year they collected to themselves whatever understanding she could bring to them at a given time. They gathered like the fallen leaves of autumn after autumn, and pressed each other down at the bottom of her mind. But they were *there,* articulated and remembered, ready for her understanding when it was ready for them. It was as if she were riven from the top of her head to the ground she stood on, and pinned there with the sharp, unbending stave of reality. She could not even turn her head to look away. Already, at ten, at twelve, at fourteen, she could not look away; she could not make her world seem other than it was. She was an accurate transcript of the surface of all she took part in. She

did not yet know how to use her reality. Even the pain of her embarrassment was without value to her; she was simply unable not
to see.

Charlie had declined the pecans and whiskey, and now he got
up and went into the kitchen. She heard the sounds of the icebox
door opening and closing, and then the creak of the hinges on the
kitchen safe. "Can I fix you a sandwich, Mrs. A., Sarah D.?" he
called.

"No thanks."

"I just can't mix whiskey and sugar," he said. "It ruins good
whiskey for me."

"Every man to his own taste," Kate said, "as the old lady said
when she kissed the cow."

"What's that?"

If I asked Gran to explain it all to me, Anna thought, *I reckon she'd
try. What I don't see is, if they all think he's so awful, why aren't they
happy now he's gone.*

Another fragmentary memory stirred in her troubled mind and
she heard the telephone ringing as she had drifted into sleep one
night, and her father's slow, gruff "All *right,*" as he answered. *That
must have been the year before Sis and Alderan moved in with us, or it
would have happened in Eureka,* she thought. "Charlotte," she heard
her father say, and she knew he must have his hand on her mother's
shoulder, shaking her to rouse her, holding her hearing aid ready in
the other hand. There was a murmur of conversation, and then her
father raised his voice, and she heard him clearly, "I said, she said

Sis has had a miscarriage." And then her mother's distressed voice answering, "Oh, *Ralph*, not *again*."

That was all. Somewhere in those brief memories lay buried the secret of what had happened.

And then there was that other time, about the telephone, she thought, *when Sis cried.*

It rang again, this time late in the afternoon while she and Sis were sitting together in the living room reading. Sis answered and it was Alderan calling long distance. "Do you *have* to?" she heard her say. And then, after a silence, "But, darling, couldn't you drive home late? Even if you didn't get here until ten or eleven, it would be better than not coming." And then, "Yes, yes, of *course* I understand. It's just that I miss you so."

But after she had hung up, Sis had begun to cry, sitting, little and huddled, in Father's old green easy chair, and Anna, in a passion of sympathy and bewilderment, had flung her arms around her and said over and over again, "*I* love you, Sis. Please don't cry. *I* love you."

Had Sis known even then that Alderan loved another lady? That was a long time before they got the divorce.

"I just missed it," Charlie was saying. "If I had been able to convince Will Strickland that it was a good thing, we'd have picked up five or six thousand dollars, just like that." He snapped his fingers. "Just like that."

Kate sighed. "Um-hum," she said, and worked out an embedded

bit of pecan with her nut pick. "Sarah D., come help us, you lazy sinner. My fingers are giving out. And you, too, Anna."

"Let us finish our stories, Mama," Sarah D. said. "We'll come in a minute."

"I never yet met a banker who could see beyond the end of his nose," Charlie said. "They'll hang on to their money till hell freezes over." He stuffed the last bite of his sandwich into his mouth and chewed slowly and thoughtfully. "Curious thing about bankers," he said. "They don't seem to realize they're in business to lend money. You'd have thought I was asking him to do me a favor, instead of putting him in the way of a little business."

"Well, there's not much loose money to hand out, these days," Kate said.

"Oh, he's *got* it," Charlie said. "Don't you worry, he's got it. He just doesn't know when to turn it loose." He put his hands in his pockets and tilted back in the frail dining room chair.

"Tilt down, Charlie," Kate said. "You'll break that little chair."

Obediently he tilted forward onto four legs. "Now, something just struck me," he said thoughtfully. "Ralph's got plenty of credit. If I could put this thing across to him, between us we could probably scare up the money." His face lit up happily. "Just think, Mrs. A.," he said, "we could buy back the house, at least make a start on it."

Sarah D. closed *The Delineator,* got up, came over to the table, and leaned on Charlie's shoulder. "We can't ask Ralph for money,

Charlie," she said, "not even for a good investment. We can't ask Ralph for any favors."

"Favors!" Charlie said. "I'd be doing him a favor if I let him in on this. Come on, baby, and help us."

Sarah D. sat down and picking up a pecan examined it thoughtfully. "I don't think Ralph can stretch his credit any farther than it's stretched," she said. "You forget how many places his money has to be put. It's a miracle he could get the credit to get started again, after Mr. Wilcox took bankruptcy and they had that trouble with Alderan."

"I know exactly how old Ralph gets his credit," Charlie said. "Have you met Rife McKay, the president of the Farmers' Trust over there?"

Sarah D. shook her head and Charlie laughed delightedly. "Well," he said, "when they met, it must have been love at first sight. He's Ralph all over again. Presbyterian elder, on the school board, loves to hunt. He even has that 'Ha, ha, ha' belly laugh like Ralph's. And he's the only man I know besides Ralph that I'd be ashamed to tell a dirty joke to. (Not that they'd refuse to listen, mind you. I don't mean that. They're just too—too pure.) Anyway, after the way Ralph behaved in that bankruptcy proceeding, I betcha old McKay'd lend him the whole bank if he asked for it."

"What's a bankruptcy proceeding?" Anna asked.

"Charlie, you shouldn't talk like that in front of the child," Kate said.

"She's not a child," Charlie said. "She's a half-grown woman. Aren't you, sweetheart? And I haven't said a word about her daddy I wouldn't say to Charlotte or to anyone."

"Charlie," Sarah D. said, "I don't know whether you know it or not, and it's strictly in the family, but Ralph has had the whole support of Miss Celestine and Miss Julia ever since the Hibernia Bank failure. And he's so hardheaded he won't get them out of that huge, expensive old house and into a sensible little apartment, so he's pouring money down a rat hole out there. I guess Waldo sends his mother a little something when he can, but James is hardly able to take care of his own family, and I know the McGovern place is just barely paying its taxes. Besides that, Ralph sends Mama thirty-five dollars every month. He has a wife and three children to support, he's up to his ears in McGovern and Wilcox debts, and he's trying to get a new business started. We simply can't ask him for anything else."

"What's a bankruptcy proceeding?" Anna asked again.

"Besides which," Sarah D. said, "it was Alderan's shenanigans that finished off McGovern and Wilcox. I think we'd better give Ralph a little breather as far as in-laws are concerned."

"Are you putting me in the class with Alderan?" Charlie asked, "When I'm sitting here faithfully picking out pecans and minding my own business?" He grinned at her.

"No, sweetie, I'm not. I'm just saying Ralph has got enough *family* to choke a horse. Have you forgotten that Sis doesn't even speak to him if she can help it?"

"All right, all right, I give up," Charlie said, "but you mark my words, somebody's going to make big money out of that."

"What's a bankruptcy proceeding?" Anna said.

"When your business fails," Sarah D. said, "and you don't have any money to pay your debts, the law lets you do something that's called 'taking bankruptcy.' That means that the people you owe money to can divide whatever you have, what are called your assets, among them, and then they can't try to make you pay any more. It's a way for people who are hopelessly in debt to get a new start."

"Did Father do that?" Anna asked.

"Anna," Kate said, "haven't you heard your mother and father talking about all that? Didn't you ask *them* about it?"

Anna shook her head. "How could I ask them when I didn't even know what to ask them about?" she said.

Sarah D. laughed. "They probably never even thought about telling you," she said. "I don't guess they thought you'd be interested. But I'm sure your mother would tell you if you asked. What happened was that Mr. Wilcox took bankruptcy, and since he was your father's partner, your father was liable for his debts. Do you know what I'm talking about?"

Anna nodded.

"But your father didn't want to do that. In other words, he didn't want to say that he wouldn't pay all his debts as soon as he was able to pay them. Under the law there is nothing wrong with it, but it seemed wrong to him. So he'll have to pay all the debts of the partnership."

The front door banged and they heard Sis's step in the parlor, quick and firm and light. She came into the dining room, pulling off her gloves and hat and smiling her small, crooked smile. She said hello to everyone in her quiet, controlled voice, and then hovered over the fire, shivering. "It's too cold for any use," she said.

"How was the movie?" Sarah D. said.

Anna did not need Sarah D.'s warning glance to know that the subject of conversation would be changed, that they were not to mention what they had been talking about. *You'd think she would look different, wouldn't you?* she said to herself. *You'd think it would show.* She examined Sis carefully, her slight, frail body, her neatly waved, short, graying brown hair, the tiny wrinkles in her soft, dry skin, her wide, thin, sad mouth, her worn tweed suit and shirtwaist, fastened at the collar with an onyx brooch. She looked just as she had always looked.

I'll bet you never saw your father look like this, Alderan said.

Oh, Ralph, not again, her mother said.

I *love you,* she said to Sis, weeping by the telephone. I *love you.*

Anna came back to the dining room and heard Sis say, "We didn't go after all. Caroline wanted to call on Miss Lucy and Miss Sally and take their Christmas presents, so we went down there and visited awhile."

"How are Lucy and Sally?" Kate asked.

"Poor old things," Sis said. "Shut up in the house together, and you know they never have gotten along. Mama, Miss Sally is pitiful. She's getting blinder by the day, and Miss Lucy is so cross with her—even when we were there, she was cross, so you know when they're alone, she must lead her a dog's life."

"Come on, Sis, and help us pick out pecans," Charlie said. "Mrs. A. and I have been trying to get your lazy sister to help us for an hour."

Sis sat down at the table and began to shell nuts. She sat straight and worked rapidly and with every nutmeat that dropped into the bowl the tension in the warm, smoky room grew tighter.

Sarah D. got up restlessly. "All right, all right, I give up," she said. "Come on, Anna, you help, too. We'll get them all picked out tonight, and then, Mama, you can get them wrapped and in the mail tomorrow."

"Have you made the list?" Kate said.

They all began to talk at once.

"Well, we want to send some to Jane Richardson. And then there are Ralph and Charlotte's, and Will and Eunice's, and I'd like to send Carrie a box. You know she always sends my Charlotte something handsome for Christmas."

"How about Bill Dupré, Charlie?"

"And the Harper girls, and—"

"I'd like to give some to Caroline."

"Hey, wait a minute, wait a minute," Charlie said. "I've already worn my hands down to the finger bones. We'll be picking 'em out for another week, at that rate."

"Never mind about Caroline," Sis said stiffly. "I'll pick some out for her."

"Come on, now, Sis," Charlie said good-naturedly, "I was only kidding."

"Well, it's the most brilliant idea we ever had for Christmas," Kate said, looking around anxiously at her family and then smiling encouragingly at Sis. "Look how many we've got, and the tree is still loaded. I can get a little nig to thrash it tomorrow for a quarter and we can pick up another twenty or thirty pounds. We shouldn't have to buy presents for anyone but the children."

"Have you seen the sweater Sis is knitting for little Ralph, Anna?" Sarah D. said. "Let me show you."

Sis continued to shell nuts, her head bent over the bowl so that her face was hidden.

"She hasn't seen the scrapbook you made for him, either," Kate said. "Get that."

Sarah D. started into the front bedroom and Charlie cautioned her, "Shhh. Don't wake Charlotte and the baby." In a few minutes she came back with an almost completed sweater and an enormous scrapbook made of bright red Indianhead, the edges pinked and the back fastened with a silk tassel. RALPH'S BOOK, the cover said in big letters cut from newspaper headlines, and below the title was a picture from the cover of a *Saturday Evening Post* of a little boy gazing passionately into the eyes of a dirty, feisty-looking dog. She laid it on the table beside Anna. "Now, you mustn't tell when you get home," she said. "It's a surprise."

"Oh! it's just like Ralph and Bo," Anna cried. "Won't he love it?"

Inside was the story of Ralph's life in pictures cut from old magazines, accompanied by silly poems composed by Sarah D. Anna giggled over the pictures and poems, and then began to examine the sweater.

Sis looked up. "I dropped a stitch in there, and it's a little bit messy," she said, pointing to the waistband with her nutpick.

"I think it's beautiful," Anna said.

"Just wait till you see what I have for you, dearie," Sis said. "You'd never guess what it is in a thousand years."

Creak, crack. Creak, crack. Creak, crack. The nutcracker groaned and the pecans exploded rhythmically into the bowl in Charlie's lap. Sis shelled her pile faster and faster. Everyone was quiet for a few minutes, and then the nervous compulsion to talk, to draw Sis out of herself, struck them all again.

"Well, Sis, what did Caroline have to say for herself?" Kate said. "Did she know any gossip?"

Charlie got up and started for the kitchen again. "Anybody want a drink of water?" he said. "Sis, can I get you a glass of milk?"

"No, thank you," she said. "No, Mama, she didn't know a thing."

The door from the dining room into the front bedroom opened slowly and they all looked up. Billy Dupré in a draggled cotton nightgown, his cheeks rosy with sleep, an old piece of blanket clutched in his round baby arms, stood there, blinking in the light.

"Did I hear someone call me?" he said in a businesslike voice.

Charlie, on his way to the kitchen, stopped, burst into a roar of laughter and went to pick him up. "It was me, Billy Boy," he said, holding him tight and kissing the top of his head. "I just couldn't live without you another minute."

"I thought it was Santa Claus," he said. "Isn't it Christmas yet?"

Charlie sat down at the table with his son and gave him a pecan. "Next week," he said. "You've got another week to wait."

"You're going to give that child a stomachache," Kate said, "feeding him pecans at this time of night."

"Don't worry, Mama," Sarah D. said. "His stomach's made of cast iron."

Sis put down her nutpick and shoved aside the bowl of pecans. "Come to me, Billy," she said, holding out her arms. "Come, sit in Sis's lap a minute."

Charlie let him go and he climbed into Sis's lap and lay back sleepily against her shoulder. "Is it tomorrow?" he asked.

Sis put both arms around the child and laid her cheek against his soft hair. "Just about, baby. Why don't you shut your eyes and take a little nap, and in a minute it'll be tomorrow."

The child sat up and frowned at Sis. "You're too bony," he said. "You stick me awake." He climbed down and went over to his mother.

Anna opened her mouth to laugh, but then she looked at Sis and saw the expression on her face, and closed it again. Sarah D. picked Billy up and began to pat his back and sing softly.

> "The sons of the prophet are brave men and bold,
> And quite unaccustomed to fear,
> But the bravest by far in the ranks of the Shah
> Was Abdul the Bulbul Amir."

Charlie got up again. "Well," he said, "I'm still thirsty. Water, anyone?"

"Why don't you drink a glass of milk, Sis?" Kate said. "You're getting entirely too thin."

"No, *thank* you, Mama," Sis said, "I'm not hungry." She had begun to work again, and she spoke without looking up.

"That's a funny song to sing to a baby," Anna said. "Does he like it?"

"He's *crazy* about it," Sis said. "Isn't that absurd?"

"But you ought to eat more," Kate said. "You really should."

Sarah D. frowned at Kate and shook her head, still patting Billy and singing softly.

> "Vile infidel, know, you have trod on the toe
> Of Abdul the Bulbul Amir."

In the kitchen Charlie began to hum, "Ta tah, *dum*, tah, *dum*, tah, *dum*," and then to whistle clearly and penetratingly above Sarah D.'s soft tuneless voice a popular song a few seasons old, "In the Valley of the Moon." Anna was leaning on her elbows watching Sis's quick fingers. "I just wish I could shell pecans or peel shrimp as fast as you can," she said.

Sis did not look up, and Anna, watching her fast-moving hands, had the curious sensation that they were the only part of her that was alive. She looked at Gran and Sarah D. and they, too, were as motionless and tense as statues. Sarah D. had stopped singing. Billy was asleep.

Everyone seemed to be listening to something, but the only sound in the house, except for the loud ticking of the clock, was Charlie's whistling in the kitchen. He began to sing, over and over the only line he knew, "Ta, tah, *dum*, tah, *dum*, tah, *dum*. In the valley of the moon."

Gran and Sarah D. both started talking.

"Sis, I wish you would . . ."

"Mama, when you go to market in the morning . . ."

"Excuse me," Sis said quietly, politely. She got up and without looking at anyone started up the stairs, not walking fast and lightly as she always did, but slowly and carefully, looking down at each riser as if she were expecting to stumble over a monster or a pot of gold.

When she was gone Sarah D. and Kate looked at each other, and then Kate closed her eyes, rested her forehead on her hands, and sighed.

Charlie came back into the room, still singing.

"Hush," Sarah D. said sharply. She sat quite still so as not to disturb the sleeping baby.

"Huh?"

"Shhh."

He stood in the doorway, bewildered. "What's the matter with you?" he said. "What's going on?"

Kate did not even open her eyes.

Anna picked up Sarah D.'s magazine and looked down at it unseeing, pretending to read. Her heart pounded with anxiety.

"Charlie, how *could* you?" Sarah D. whispered fiercely. "How *could* you?"

"Honey, I don't even know what you're talking about," he said.

"That *song*," Sarah D. said. "Don't you know that was Alderan's song?"

Charlie looked around and saw that Sis was gone. "Well, for God's sake," he said. "Of all the damn foolishness. If she can't listen to a damn song!"

"Just try to be careful, Charlie," Sarah D. said. "When you're around her try to be careful, will you?"

Charlie turned ruefully to Anna. "You see how it is, honey," he said. "I'm snakebit. I can't *ever* do anything right."

"Oh, *Charlie*," Sarah D. said.

"But I was just trying to help. How was I to know she'd get upset? I was just trying to cheer us up. That's all. I'm getting so I'm scared to open my mouth around here."

Upstairs they heard the water gurgling down the drain in a flood.

"What's she trying to do, wash herself away?" Charlie said.

Kate picked up a piece of newspaper and braced it stiffly against the side of the table for a dustpan. She swept a pile of loose pecan shells into it and dumped them into the paper under the nutcracker. "Go to bed, all of you," she said. "Go on to bed. I'll clean up." She touched Sarah D. lightly on the shoulder. "Maybe tomorrow will be a better day," she said.

Merry Christmas, Scotty

by Larry Brown

I was sitting in the bar, watching it snow, and enjoying my very last merry Christmas cup of eggnog. I'd seen Sammy throw the empty carton into the garbage already, and I hadn't seen him make a move to send an interning bartender booking out east to Kroger for another one, probably because the place was almost deserted anyway, as it should have been, since it was Christmas Eve, and late, and the snow was already deep.

Oh sure, there'd been some holiday rounds bought earlier, and some off-key yodeling of Christmas carols, along with plenty of eggnog-quaffing, but that bundled-up brood of hearty backslappers, all bedecked with wrapped presents hot from Neilson's or Fred's, had already slung their mufflers around their necks and hit the door on the way to fur-lined Noel's nests with warm loved ones, probably to get some presents unwrapped and give them to each other early, Ho Ho Hoing all the way down the stairs. So it was pretty quiet in there. And you see things and you try not to think about them too much, but some bald-headed white-bearded guy had had his head on the bar a few stools down for quite a while, and it was a cinch he wasn't Santa Claus. Santa didn't wear

Gucci loafers or lambswool sweaters, and he didn't pass out in bars. Santa was a retired biker, a Tough Love old dude who lived up at the North Pole, and worked hard, and he and his little elves hammered and sawed and painted presents for all the children of the world, and then once a year he pulled on his colors, and took the reins in his teeth beside that stubby meerschaum pipe, and cracked the whip smartly above the frosted backs of his standing team blowing steam, and then mushed them up into the sky and went south to Alaska just for starters, the cold air blowing in his face, and all of us spread out here below him. But Santa was for kids, and I wasn't a kid anymore, even though at one time I had been and still remembered how cool it had been, like being able to crawl around under tables while people were eating and nobody thinking anything about it. Or fall into a small ball and just roll.

I really wanted some more of that eggnog. Sammy had been kind enough to lace it for me with some old mead he'd been keeping cool in a storeroom downstairs somewhere just for this, just for Christmas. But now that the place had almost cleared out, I knew that Sammy could probably slow down and reflect a little on the past year and how it had gone and even have a glass of that tasty mead-spiced concoction himself, which is just what he did after he threw the carton away.

He moved down to where I was sitting. He smiled at me, hefted up his glass. I hoisted my cup. We knocked the rims together gently and sipped a little more.

After he wiped a big eggnog mustache off his upper lip, Sammy said: "You glad to be home for Christmas, Nick?"

"Sure am," I said. "We ain't got any more of that eggnog left back there, have we?"

He shook his head sadly and looked down at the glass. "Sure don't, Nick. Sure wish we did. But listen here. We could play some music."

"Yeah. We sure could. Maybe they've got some Christmas songs back there."

"Maybe so," he said, and he went to the big CD jukebox at the back, over near the porch. I could see the snow still coming down past the windows. I saw him give the old guy on the bar a glance as he went by him and I wondered what Sammy was going to have to do with him or to him to get him eventually out of there. I myself already had a pretty good spot at the Hotty Totty Motel, over on North Lamar, out there where Mr. Norris's Phillips 66 used to be. It wasn't really a room. They'd run out of rooms since so many people had come home for Christmas and wanted rooms, so the only thing they'd been able to offer me without a reservation was a tent. And even though it was in the parking lot, they'd been kind enough to run me a couple of power cords out there along with a cable, so I had a regular room TV with a channel changer and everything, so it wasn't too bad, just had kind of a hard floor for camping and occasional traffic noise. And now that the snow had piled up around it and some over it, it was kind of nice and warm in there under my electric blanket. I'd put a toy Christmas tree on top of the TV like a sap. It had only cost me two dollars at a rummage sale I'd walked by a day or two before, and it was small and all, but still it had been giving me a bit of Christmas joy. I knew there were plenty of people in the world who were getting plenty out of Christmas. And they were supposed to. That's what Christmas was for, man.

Christmas was all about Baby Jesus and pumpkin pie and good smells in a well-known kitchen and shiny little eyes, and it was magic somehow, how it kept coming around each year and renewing the hopes and dreams for peace on earth for God's sake? Finally? Please? Christmas kept coming around because it had good reasons for coming around, and it was hard even if you had little not to be a little bit happy. I'd even bought myself a few presents, a pair of black nylon socks for one, and one of those six-packs of hankies that are only like a buck apiece, and I had a box of chocolate-covered cherries wrapped up, and a few apples and oranges were sitting in a bowl beside them, all of it piled up on top of the TV. So it wasn't going to be a bad Christmas.

"You got something you want to hear, Nick?" Sammy called from the machine back there.

I thought about it for a moment, and then I said: "Yeah, man, you got that 'Blue Christmas' number old Leon Russell did, is it on there?"

Sammy looked for a long time. I kept watching the snow through the windows and thinking about how cold it was going to be out there. I wondered what the old guy was going to do. The streets were bad, and even the police had to be creeping, and I didn't know if the old guy was walking or driving, but it didn't really matter because either way he was probably going to be up the creek without a paddle.

Just dashing through the snow on my way up from the Hotty Totty, my nose had almost run, and it had weirded me out to see the courthouse lawn blanketed in white, and to see how empty the streets were. Sammy looked up and shook his head.

"Sorry, Nick, I don't believe it's on here."

I thought some more. "How about 'Merry Christmas Baby' by Lightnin' Hopkins, he really bends some strings on that one, man."

Sammy looked some more and he stayed quiet back there for a long time. I felt like if I could just get one more cup of that eggnog inside me before I had to go back out into the snow, I might be able to face my Christmas the next morning.

"Gee, Nick, you know what? I don't think there's any Christmas songs on this jukebox. I guess the CD guy forgot to bring 'em in and put 'em in the machine. We got Santana."

I didn't say anything and Sammy went back to looking at the CDs. I sipped a little more from my cup. I couldn't help glancing at the old guy. He didn't have any wet circles or empty glasses around him. I figured Sammy had already cleared the mess away, probably afraid he'd knock something off and break it if he came to and didn't know where he was or fell off the bar stool.

Looking at him got me to thinking about all the Christmases I'd seen come and go. I remembered a train set and a piece of track I'd cut my finger on Christmas morning, and I remembered a brightly lit tree in front of rippled wallpaper in a dimly lighted living room, and my little brother in one of those crazy little brother bathrobes, and then a real early Christmas when my Uncle Freddy had brought in a humongous frozen turkey that seemed in my memory to have covered the whole kitchen table, and my aunts, my daddy's sisters, laughing with him, my grandaddy there with us when he was still alive, all those years ago when my own eyes had been shiny and little.

"I think I'll just put some Al Green on," Sammy said, and I nodded, and pretty soon Al was meaning and growling through the big speakers back there. And I was thinking of how right Sammy's wisdom was, of how listening to a little Al always seemed to make you feel better, no matter what the season.

Sammy headed back across the floor, and then he stopped to pick up a couple of chairs and turn them upside down on a table. He looked at the old guy again, and then he came on back to where I was and pulled up a bar stool and sat down beside me.

"What you gonna do about him?" I said.

"Let him sleep," Sammy said. "He's probably pretty tired."

I wondered if maybe the old guy didn't have anybody to go home to, or anybody to come take care of him. And it was so cold out there, if he was walking, he might get frostbite toe, if he couldn't move fast enough to get someplace where he could get inside and get warm.

"Yeah," I said. "It's been a long Christmas season already. I know people get tired of doing all that shopping. I bet you can barely get around out at Wally-World for all the pushing and shoving and shopping-cart collisions."

"Hey man," Sammy said. "I heard they had so many fistfights with people trying to get inside they had to put the mall cops on skateboards."

For a while we just sat at the bar and watched it snow through the windows. It kept falling in big flakes and some of them stuck to the glass and then slid slowly down. Big Al kept wailing back there, and inside it felt just like home. I knew the paintings on the walls, and the boards in the floor, and the bottles at the back in front of the mirror were like old friends. And it shouldn't have mattered that I didn't have anybody to spend Christmas with, but it did. I didn't know the old guy who was passed out, didn't know if maybe he was one of those people who wanted to try and tell you what you were about, or who started out nice and then got nasty after a couple of drinks, or stole your cigarette lighter. He might even be one of those stoned-acting guys who wanted to talk to you while real loud music or a band was playing and kept shouting painfully in your ear a bunch of stuff that you already knew. It was also entirely possible that he had somebody waiting for him some-where, in a house, and it was all decorated with Christmas deco-rations, with a real tree and tinsel, and presents in boxes with shiny paper and bows, presents that rattled or shook when you picked them up and gave them a shake, or were only kind of heavy and didn't rattle or shake at all and didn't give you any indication of what they might be. He might even, in his refrigerator, have a tall waxed carton of that old Christmas cream hiding in there himself.

"Boy," I said to Sammy. "Another cup of that eggnog would sure be good. Kind of a one for the old Christmas road thing, know what I mean, Sammy?"

"Yeah," he said. "I know what you mean, Nick. It'd be a bad trip down to James' Food Center in this snow, though. If they're even open. It looks like it's coming a real blizzard out there."

I looked out the window again and he was right.

It was suddenly unbelievable how hard the snow was falling.

I took my cup with me and walked over to the door on the left of the jukebox where Al was crying about how he's so tired of being alone, and it was amazing and I was amazed. You wouldn't have thought that much snow could've fallen that fast in North Mississippi. Only a few cars were still sitting on the square, but the snow had made an individual igloo out of each one of them. The parking islands were just long humps in the snow, and it didn't look like any cars had passed between the island over by Ajax and the courthouse in quite a while. I thought about the boys in the fire station, and sure hoped they wouldn't have to take their pretty red trucks out in this weather. And the sky, wow. The street lamps showed a sky full of falling flakes of snow, and they were dropping so fast and so thick and so silently . . .

What if the cops got the old guy? What would they do with him? If he was drunk and tried to drive, or was drunk and tried to walk? Would they even be out patrolling in snow this deep? And was that good or was that bad? Would it be better, if they were going to catch him, to catch him and take him to the warm jail, or would it be worse if they didn't catch him and he made it to his car and cranked it up and then was either too drunk to move it or the snow was piled up too deep to move it, and he sat there and passed out and went to sleep or something, and started doing that exhaust fume-huffing thing? And there was always the chance that he might not even be able to find his car in all that snow, and might start wandering around in that white cold stuff and get dead feet and numb fingers, and his nose might almost start running like mine did, and then he might not have any warm place to get into at all, if he couldn't stagger down the drifted sidewalks toward Four Corners, and find a gas station that was open, and that might be entirely possible, on Christmas Eve. Then what if he staggered back up the street by D'Jango's, and ducked into the one behind Smitty's, and crawled right up in Faulkner Alley and froze to death? Aw man, we'd be tainted then, or at least kissed by some bad karma, and unable to cherish the mantras of our own true natures, like Harrison suggested.

So I said to myself: Well. It ain't a whole lot of room in my Hotty Totty tent. It'd be kind of cramped up but I guess he could stay with me if he didn't start taking all the covers and pulling my electric blanket off me. Just for overnight anyway. Once he got sobered up he could probably get on to wherever he needed to go. If I could haul his drunken carcass down the street in all that snow in the first place.

So I turned around, took the last sip of my eggnog, and set the empty cup on a table close to the jukebox lights. It was showing close to midnight on the clock behind the bar, and I knew that Sammy was probably ready to go on home to his own Christmas, whatever it was going to be. His girlfriend was probably waiting for him, and they probably had stuff under the tree.

"I'll help you with him, Sammy," I said, after I got back over to the bar, and Sammy said: "Say what?"

"The old dude," I said, and pointed. I pulled my bearskin off the back of the stool I'd been sitting on and started buttoning it up. I knew that somebody had to be working at the Hotty Totty who might could get him some coffee in the lobby. "I thought I'd help you get him out on the street, make sure he don't freeze to death."

"Freeze to death?" said Sammy. "What you talking about, Nick?"

"Well," I said, "he's passed out ain't he?"

"Aw naw," he said. "That's my Uncle Kris from Crystal Springs. He just flew back from Australia for Christmas and he had to drive through all that snow from Memphis right before they closed the roads down. He's got jet lag."

"Oh," I said.

He leaned over and screamed in the old guy's ear: "Hey Uncle Kris! Rise and shine, baby! It's Christmas!"

And like a preprogrammed robot, the old guy lifted his head from the bar and looked around alertly and said: "Is the house on fire? Where's my slippers? What time is it?"

He got off his stool and Sammy introduced us and he shook my hand with a firm hearty handshake and in just a minute the lights were shut off and we were bustling down the stairs to the street. Sammy locked the door behind us and we stood there for just a small amount of time and looked around. There was not a creature stirring in that white and silent landscape around the square. There was nothing but the snow falling, and falling, and falling. His uncle talked about Australia and climbing Ayers Rock, and Sammy shoved his hands deep into his pockets and tried to keep the snowflakes from falling into his collar.

"Well," I said, "it's nice meeting you, Kris, and Sammy, both of you, have a good Christmas. I got to get back over to the Hotty Totty."

"I thought they were sold out," Sammy said.

"Well, they had one spot left," I said, and I shook hands with both of them and started to head over by Uncle Buck's. I thought if I stayed under those awnings on that side of the square I could make it pretty easy until I had to cross the street over by the Downtown Grill.

And then I heard Sammy call my name. I turned.

"Don't leave just yet, Nick, come on and go to a Christmas party with us. Uncle Kris just bought him one of these cool balcony apartments right across the street. We got plenty of eggnog over there, all kind of stuff to eat, and I know we've got some Christmas songs. There's about thirty people over there just waiting on me to get off work."

"Well. Boy. Okay," I said, and we waded through the snow at the corner of Square Books and made some snowballs and threw them at each other climbing up the stairs that led across the roof of Proud Larry's. We could hear the music before we even got in. And once we got in, it was packed with people and Christmas tunes and noise and light. People I hadn't seen in a while hugged me, and it was warm, and it was cozy, and within two minutes I had another cup of eggnog in my hand and was talking to a long-legged brown-haired beauty named Desiree who had just moved down here from New York City and was tired of boys and wanted a man who could show her the Oxford ropes.

I said: "Well, all I've got is some tent ropes," and she said that sounded like a good place to start.

I said: "Well, that snow's kind of deep and it's about a block and a half down there," and she said she was used to walking fourteen blocks of snow in New York City.

And I said: "Well, I don't have any music down there, but I do have a TV," and she said she knew for a fact that some station would be showing either *It's a Wonderful Life* or *A Christmas Story* or *Miracle on Thirty-fourth Street,* and I said: "You know what? I bet Sammy would let us take a whole carton of that eggnog along with us," and you know what? He did.

Merry Christmas, everybody.

Contributors

Doris Betts, a native of Statesville, North Carolina, began her writing career working for the *Statesville Daily Record.* She has published nine books of fiction, including *Beasts of the Southern Wild and Other Stories, Heading West,* and *Souls Raised from the Dead,* which won the Southern Book Award and was named one of the Twenty Best Books of 1994 by the *New York Times.* In addition, she has won the 1998 North Caroliniana Society Award, the Presbyterian Writers Guild Award, the North Carolina Humanities Council's John Tyler Caldwell Award, the John Dos Passos Prize, and is a three-time winner of the Sir Walter Raleigh Award and holder of the Medal of Merit in the Short Story from the American Academy of Arts and Letters. She retired in 2002 as Alumni Distinguished Professor of English at the University of North Carolina at Chapel Hill, where a chaired professorship in her name is currently held by novelist Pam Durban. She lives with her husband on a farm near Pittsboro, North Carolina.

Larry Brown was born in Oxford, Mississippi, in 1951. He served two years in the Marine Corps and sixteen years in the Oxford Fire Department, changing careers in 1990 to write full time. His books have won many prizes and awards, and have been translated into languages around the world. His ninth book, a novel called *The Rabbit Factory,* was released in September 2003 by the Free Press.

Ellen Douglas (Josephine Haxton), born in Natchez, Mississippi, is a graduate of the University of Mississippi. She is the author of eight novels, two of which, *A Family's Affairs* and *Black Cloud, White Cloud,* were included in the *New York Times Book Review*'s Year's Ten Best listings. *A Family's Affairs* received a Houghton Mifflin Fellowship. Her fourth novel, *Apostles of Light,* was a finalist for the National Book Award. Her latest work, *Truth: Four Stories I Am Finally Old Enough to Tell,* was published by Algonquin Books of Chapel Hill in 1998. *Witnessing,* a collection of articles and essays from four decades, will be published in the fall by the University Press of Mississippi.

Clyde Edgerton was born in Durham, North Carolina. He received a Ph.D. from the University of North Carolina at Chapel Hill and is the author of eight novels, five of which received notable book awards from the *New York Times.* He received a Guggenheim Fellowship in 1989, the Lyndhurst Fellowship, and the 1997 North Carolina Award for Literature. He is also a noted musician and has taught at Duke University, the University of North Carolina at Chapel Hill, and Millsaps College. He is currently a professor of creative writing at the University of North Carolina at Wilmington.

Kaye Gibbons was twenty-eight when her first novel, *Ellen Foster,* was published. Walker Percy hailed it as "a lovely, sometimes heart-wrenching novel," while Eudora Welty called Gibbons "a stunning new writer." Six more novels followed, each gathering prizes and accolades. *Divining Women* is her seventh, the first to appear in six years. Gibbons lives in Raleigh, North Carolina, with her three daughters.

Gail Godwin was born in Alabama and grew up in Asheville, North Carolina. She received a doctorate in English at the University of Iowa and taught at Vassar College and Columbia University. She has received a Guggenheim Fellowship, National Endowment of the Arts grants for both fiction and libretto writing, and the Award in Literature from the American Academy and Institute of Arts and Letters. Three of her novels were nominated for the National Book Award: *The Odd Woman*, *Violet Clay*, and *A Mother and Two Daughters*. She has published ten novels, two collections of short fiction, and a book of nonfiction. Her most recent books are *Evensong* (1999) and *Heart: A Personal Journey through Its Myth and Meanings* (2001).

Carolyn Haines, a native of Lucedale, Mississippi, is the author of the Sarah Booth Delaney mystery series set in the Mississippi Delta. *Hallowed Bones* (2004) is the fifth and latest in the series. Haines, the recipient of an Alabama Council on the Arts writing fellowship, is also the author of two earlier novels, *Touched* and *Summer of the Redeemers*, which have been reissued in trade paperback by River City Publishing. She lives in Semmes, Alabama, and teaches creative writing at the University of South Alabama.

Donald Harington was born and raised in Little Rock, Arkansas. He is Distinguished Professor of Art History at the University of Arkansas at Fayetteville and the author of thirteen novels about the fictional Ozark Mountains town of Stay More. He was the 2003 winner of the Robert Penn Warren Award for Fiction, given in recognition of his body of work by the Fellowship of Southern Writers. He received the Heasley Prize for Literary Excellence from Lyon College; he was inducted into the Arkansas Writers Hall of Fame in 1999, and the Winter 2002 issue of *Southern Quarterly* is devoted to his work. Last spring his latest novel

With, from which "Christmas on Madewell Mountain" is taken, received critical acclaim.

Silas House was born and raised in Lily, Kentucky, and is the author of three novels, *Clay's Quilt, A Parchment of Leaves,* and *The Coal Tattoo.* He was chosen as one of the ten best emerging writers by the Millennial Gathering of Writers in 2000 and has received awards from the Fellowship of Southern Writers and the National Society of Arts and Letters. His first novel, *Clay's Quilt,* won the *ForeWord* magazine Bronze Award and was nominated for both the Southeastern Booksellers Book of the Year Award and the Appalachian Writers Association Book Award. *A Parchment of Leaves* has been nominated for the AWA Book Award and was a Top Ten Book Sense pick. A reader on National Public Radio's *All Things Considered* and a contributing editor for *No Depression* magazine, House lives in eastern Kentucky with his wife and two daughters.

Nanci Kincaid, a native of Tallahassee, Florida, has written three novels: *Crossing Blood, Balls,* and *Verbena,* and a collection of short stories, *Pretending the Bed Is a Raft.* Her short fiction has appeared in *Story, Southern Exposure, Missouri Review, Carolina Quarterly,* and *New Stories from the South.* In 1992, she received a grant from the National Endowment for the Arts, and in 1994–95 she was a Mary Ingram Bunting Fellow (Radcliffe/Harvard). Kincaid has taught fiction writing at the University of Alabama, the University of North Carolina at Charlotte, and the University of Arizona. Her short story "Pretending the Bed is a Raft" has been made into a film titled *My Life Without Me,* produced by Pedro Almodovar. She currently splits her time between Hawaii and Austin, Texas.

Michael Knight is a native of Mobile, Alabama. His fiction has appeared in the *New Yorker, Paris Review,* the *Virginia Quarterly Review, Esquire, GQ, Playboy,* and other magazines. His first two books, *Dogfight and Other Stories* and *Divining Rod,* a novel, were both published in 1998. His second collection of short stories, *Goodnight, Nobody,* was published in February 2003 by Grove/Atlantic. Knight teaches writing at the University of Tennessee.

Charline R. McCord, a resident of Clinton, Mississippi, was born in Hattiesburg and grew up in Laurel, Mississippi, and Jackson, Tennessee. She holds bachelor's and master's degrees in English from Mississippi College, where she won the Bellamann Award for Creative Writing and edited the literary magazine. She is completing doctoral work at the University of Southern Mississippi on contemporary Southern women writers. McCord is Associate Director of PIRE's Southeast Center for the Application of Prevention Technologies, and a part-time instructor of English. She has published poetry, short fiction, interviews, book reviews, and feature articles. In 2001, she contributed to and coedited *Christmas Stories from Mississippi* and in 2003 she coedited *A Very Southern Christmas.*

Jill McCorkle, a native of Lumberton, North Carolina, received degrees from the University of North Carolina and Hollins College. The author of five novels and three collections of short stories, her books have been chosen four times for the *New York Times* Notable Books of the Year list, and her fiction was selected in 1988, 1991, 1993, and 1996 for *New Stories from the South.* She is the recipient of the New England Book Award, the North Carolina Award for Literature, and the John Dos Passos Prize for fiction. She has taught at Duke, Tufts, Harvard, Bennington, and the University of North Carolina. McCorkle currently resides in Massachusetts.

Judy H. Tucker, a sixth-generation Mississippian, is a freelance writer, a playwright, and a book reviewer for *Planet Weekly* in Jackson, Mississippi. She contributed to and coedited *Christmas Stories from Mississippi* and coedited *A Very Southern Christmas*. This is her fifth collaboration with artist Wyatt Waters.

Wyatt Waters was born in Brookhaven, Mississippi, grew up in Florence, and moved to Clinton, Mississippi, in the tenth grade. He holds bachelor's and master's degrees in art from Mississippi College, where he won the Bellamann Award for Art and Creative Writing. Waters frequently teaches art classes in the Jackson area and has had solo shows at the Mississippi Museum of Art and the Lauren Rogers Museum of Art in Laurel. He has published three books of his paintings, *Another Coat of Paint, Painting Home,* and *An Oxford Sketchbook,* and has illustrated *Christmas Stories from Mississippi, A Southern Palette,* and *A Very Southern Christmas.* He was commissioned to do commemorative posters for Jackson's Jubilee! Jam, the Crossroads Film Festival, and Washington, D.C.'s Mississippi on the Mall. His work has been featured in numerous magazine articles, including *American Artists Special Watercolor Issues, Art and Antiques,* and *Mississippi Magazine,* and he was the recipient of the Visual Artist Award from the Mississippi Institute of Arts and Letters in 2004. His gallery is located on Jefferson Street in Olde Towne Clinton. His work is also available for viewing at www.wyattwaters.com.

Acknowledgments

SURELY THERE CAN be no better time or place to thank those who have bestowed great, yearlong gifts on us than *now*, at Christmastime, and *here*, in the pages of a book that has moved from fantasy to reality thanks to the combined efforts of many. It gives us great joy to champion here our many benefactors. We are deeply indebted to our editor at Algonquin, Kathy Pories, who has gifted us with good humor, great patience, keen insight, and unrelenting professionalism as we've navigated the course of publishing two books together. We are most appreciative to our publisher, Elisabeth Scharlatt, for believing in the value of this project and for the invaluable role she played in guiding it to fruition. We repeat and stress our sincere gratitude to Shannon Ravenel and Lee Smith, who were there in the beginning and who played a large part in bringing us into the Algonquin fold.

We owe an enormous debt to John Evans, owner of Lemuria bookstore in Jackson, Mississippi, for regularly taking time from his busy schedule to share with us an independent bookseller's knowledge and experience of what works and why it works — a knowledge so acute that we've come to think of him as the Alan Greenspan of bookselling. We express equal appreciation to Thomas Miller, Lemuria's manager, and to the entire Lemuria staff, for their ongoing encouragement and numerous acts of kindness and support. We also thank Marian Young and Carolyn Haines for their friendship and the knowledge they have shared about the book industry, and James Patterson for his loyal support and encouragement and his skilled photography.

We are grateful to the eleven writers represented in this collection — writers whose unique stories of Christmas help us understand what a consistently complex holiday December 25th really is. We continue to marvel at the uncommon talent of Wyatt Waters, but we also value Wyatt for the great friend that he is and as a fellow conspirator in all that we have attempted to bring to life here. In addition, we sing the praises of his lovely wife, Vicki, for her abiding friendship and her capable promotion and ongoing involvement with our books.

We salute the employees of the law firm of Brunini, Grantham, Grower & Hewes, Union Planters Bank, and other great patrons of the arts, who support fine literature. And a special thanks goes to our family, friends, and readers; many have sent us holiday greetings and good wishes, and others have turned up at the most unexpected times and places to cheer us on.

Finally, from the bottom of our hearts, we wish to thank the countless booksellers who promote and sell our books. Many of you made Christmas more memorable by inviting us into your bookstores for signings, which often swelled into gala events where holiday spirits soared, where you rolled out a red carpet of Southern hospitality, where you, your friends, and neighbors gathered us in like long-lost relatives who'd finally come home for the holidays. There is no better Christmas gift than that. Yet, most of you looked around and found some other Christmas favor to bestow before walking us to the door and urging, "Y'all come back now." Don't worry, we plan to. Christmas simply wouldn't be the same without you now.

Copyright Acknowledgments